Cousins of Reform:

Elizabeth Cady Stanton and Gerrit Smith

Norman K. Dann

LOG CABIN BOOKS

Cousins of Reform:

Elizabeth Cady Stanton and Gerrit Smith

Norman K. Dann

Log Cabin Books
Hamilton, NY 13346
www.logcabinbooks.us

First Edition: March 2013
10 9 8 7 6 5 4 3 2 1

ISBN   978-0-9848911-15

Library of Congress Control Number: 2013934204

The publisher will donate a portion
of the sale of this book to the
National Abolition Hall of Fame & Museum
and to the National Women's Hall of Fame.

To Wendy Lynn Dann,
whose optimism and perseverance
in the face of crushing discouragement
provide an inspiring model to us all.

Contents

PREFACE

*"The prolonged slavery of woman is the darkest page
in human history."*
—Editors of <u>History of Woman Suffrage</u>, volume I, 1889.[1]

In this first sentence of their six-volume work, the editors of the "History of Woman Suffrage"—one of whom was Elizabeth Cady Stanton—melded the two monumental issues of discrimination against African Americans and women.

Having researched the Reform Era (roughly 1820-1860) for two decades[2], I find it impossible to segregate the antislavery movement from the women's rights movement. The study of one of them leads inevitably to the other.

This book is about these two radical social reforms—the abolition of discrimination against African Americans, and the abolition of discrimination against women. As such, it will address some of the most important social issues of our time; racism and sexism are still with us in the twenty-first century. We could probably discuss without conclusion which of the two issues is most important. Because of my extensive coverage of the issue of racism in other books, the emphasis in this work is placed on sexism and the women's rights movement.

Because these two radical social reform movements overlapped for a time, and even employed some of the same leaders and participants, it makes sense to link the movements together.

This can be done through issues of human rights and through people. While the human rights issues are probably clear to most liberal-minded people today, perhaps the links among leaders are not. As one example of this crossover of leadership between the two movements, I have chosen to examine, where appropriate, the relationship between Elizabeth Cady Stanton and Gerrit Smith. Cady Stanton and Smith were both radical thinkers for their time. They were perceptive regarding the social realities that surrounded them, angry about the inequalities they perceived, and determined to dedicate their resources to the process of reweaving the social fabric into a pattern that would offer equal benefit to all people. They were both passionate, at times fanatical, eloquent, and committed reformers, and—of all things—first cousins! Their mothers were sisters in the James Livingston and Elizabeth Simpson Livingston family of eastern New York. Margaret Livingston (Cady Stanton's mother) and Elizabeth Livingston (Smith's mother) imbued both families with prestige.

This book is not an attempt to cover the entire lives of Cady Stanton and Smith; that has been done in other works.[3] I prefer to examine their lives where they intersected. Sometimes they cruised together in harmony; other times, they slammed together in crushing disagreement and criticism.

This 'dual-biography' approach affords the reader a refreshingly different view of history when compared to an 'events-and-issues' approach, or the single-person interpretation of it. I have attempted to construct a dynamic interplay of parallel lives in the hope that it may offer a more complete picture of the people and the times—and a clearer understanding of personal and societal transformations. We will see how people often reinvent themselves to meet challenges, and why a rigid description of anyone is invalid. Both the people and the times flex together, one always influencing the other. The interpersonal connections may be as important as the pressure of events when it comes to the process of shaping one's actions and beliefs. To wit: Cady Stanton became more radical as she aged due in part to the conservative changes taking place in Smith's ideas, and Smith's perception of the negative effects of religion became secularized as Cady Stanton pointed out its influence on women.

In the long run, they respected each other in spite of their disagreements, and were comfortable with each other's chastisements and advice. Importantly, they were skilled at using words—both in oration and writing. These were the most powerful communicative media of the day, and made them 'rock stars' in the worlds of influence and reform. I have used original quotes wherever possible to convey the flavor of thoughts and attitudes of the participants.

Theirs was a lifelong struggle to develop a society that could offer more equity and contentment for all people. May it serve as a model for us today.

Part I

The Reform Movements

ONE

Two Cousins

The woman's rights movement opts for "human rights—the sacred rights of a woman to her own person.... Did it ever enter into the mind of man that woman too had [the] inalienable right to life, liberty, and the pursuit of individual happiness?"
—Letter, Elizabeth Cady Stanton
to Gerrit Smith, December 21, 1855.

Elizabeth Cady was born on November 12, 1815, the eighth of eleven children born to Daniel and Margaret Livingston Cady. The siblings included five boys and six girls, all of whom were subject to the conservative gender bias of the era. Elizabeth noted when she was twenty-four,

> "It was easily seen that while my father was kind to us all, the one son [who lived to be twenty] filled a larger place in his affections and future plans than the five daughters together."[1]

As part of the Cady family, Elizabeth grew up with elite connections to the Van Rensselaers, Schuylers, Livingstons, and Smiths. Daniel Cady and Margaret Livingston married in 1801. He became a lawyer in Johnstown, New York, served one term in the United States House of Representatives, and was a justice on the New York State Supreme Court. Margaret, the daughter of James Livingston, a colonel in the Revolutionary War, was a self-confident, assertive woman who expected to be influential. She once insisted that the votes of local women be counted in the selection of a new church minister. Elizabeth had a poor relationship with her conservative father—who disapproved of her reformist attitude—and a good relationship with her liberal mother, who was proud of her daughter's challenge to male dominance.[2]

Elizabeth's education started, of course, in her home. She was tutored in liberal ideas by her brother-in-law Edward Bayard, and by a neighbor, Rev. Simon Hosack. She also saw the work and attitudes of some black servants and at least one slave. Informal "schooling" also took place in the Peterboro home of Gerrit and Ann Smith. During her summer visits there, she was introduced to abolition through Smith and his visitors, and to women's rights through the Native American connection.[3]

Formal education started at Johnstown Academy, where she studied languages and math until age fifteen. She entered Troy Female Seminary in 1831. It was there that she heard the evangelist Charles Grandison Finney speak. His ideas helped her pull away from the Calvinistic emphasis on fate and superstition and toward the ascendancy of human free will, launching her into reform activity.[4]

The reform impulse received stimulation from several directions, including her reactions to the authority of her conservative father and her house nurse, Mary Dunn. And when Edward Bayard signed on as an apprentice in Daniel Cady's law office, he attracted Elizabeth's attention to the sex bias against women that was written in law. He also persuaded Daniel to allow Elizabeth to attend Troy Female Seminary instead of having her "make puddings and pies."

After graduation from Troy, she enjoyed arguing with her father's law students in order to "make these young men recognize my equality."5

An important aspect of Cady Stanton's reform work was her colleagues, the most significant being Susan B. Anthony. In March of 1851, William Lloyd Garrison and British abolitionist George Thompson organized an antislavery meeting to be held in Seneca Falls, New York. Amelia Bloomer, editor of <u>The Lily</u>, invited Susan B. Anthony to attend, and it was there that she met Elizabeth Cady Stanton. Elizabeth would later write,

> "We were at once fast friends, in thought and sympathy we were one, and in the division of labor we exactly complemented each other. In writing we did better work together than either could alone. While she is slow and analytical in compositions, I am rapid and synthetic. I am the better writer, she the better critic. She supplied the facts and statistics, I the philosophy and rhetoric, and together we have made arguments that have stood unshaken by the storms of thirty long years: arguments that no man has answered. Our speeches may be considered the united product of our two brains."

They felt so compatible, Elizabeth noted, that "not one feeling of jealousy or envy has ever shadowed our lives."

Their friend, journalist Theodore Tilton, said of them,

> "I know of no two more pertinacious incendiaries in the whole country.... In fact this noise-making twain are the two sticks of a drum, keeping up what Daniel Webster called 'The rub-a-dub' of agitation."6

When apart, they missed each other. With the only form of communication being letters, they wrote often. When Elizabeth

acquired a new residence in New York City in 1856, she wrote to
Susan:

> "I hope in a short time to be comfortably located in a
> new house where we will have a room ready for you….
> I long to put my arms about you once more and hear
> you scold me for all my sins and shortcomings…. Oh,
> Susan, you are very dear to me. I should miss you more
> than any other living being on this earth. You are
> entwined with much of my happy and eventful past,
> and all my future plans are based on you as coadjutor.
> Yes, our work is one, we are one in aim and sympathy,
> and should be together. Come home."[7]

Lucretia Mott was also an important colleague to Cady Stanton. They met at the World Anti-Slavery Conference in London
in 1840. Each was livid over the refusal of British abolitionists
to seat them as delegates, and they agreed to plan a woman's
rights conference in the United States when they returned. "Mrs.
Mott," said Cady Stanton, "was to me an entire new revelation
of womanhood. I sought every opportunity to be at her side, and
continually plied her with questions…."

She described the meeting as an enlightening experience.
Mott stimulated Cady Stanton's reform-mindedness because
Mott would recognize "no higher authority than the judgment of
a pure-minded educated woman." Cady Stanton commented, "I
felt at once a new-born sense of dignity and freedom."

They collaborated throughout their lives on reform issues in
both the antislavery and women's rights movements, with Mott
being a model of public presence. "Mrs. Mott did not manifest
the slightest restraint or embarrassment…. No fictitious superiority ever oppressed her, neither did she descend… from her natural
dignity…."[8]

Elizabeth Smith Miller (Gerrit and Ann Smith's daughter) and Cady Stanton, at first childhood friends, remained colleagues in reform work as adults. Miller designed the "bloomer" dress reform idea that Cady Stanton adopted for a while in the 1850s. In their correspondence they called each other "Julius and Johnson," nicknames suggested by Miller's father Gerrit.

Clearly, another important person in her life was Henry Brewster Stanton. Born in Pachaug, Connecticut on June 29, 1805, he worked in his father's cargo trading business as a boy. As a young man he moved to Rochester, New York in 1826 and became a journalist with the <u>Monroe Telegraph</u>. After meeting evangelist Finney in 1830, he attended Lane Seminary to become a minister. There he helped organize the "Lane debates" over slavery, met the radical young abolitionist Theodore Dwight Weld, and dedicated his life to antislavery work. His interest in political activity to pursue the abolition of slavery brought him into contact with Gerrit Smith in 1839. In October of 1839 he was staying with the Smiths in Peterboro while on a lecture tour, and met the twenty-three year old Elizabeth Cady there.[9]

After a one-month courtship, they announced their engagement, and received opposition to it from Daniel Cady and Gerrit Smith. These two powerful men, she said, "convinced me that I was too hasty." She postponed the marriage, then decided to marry Henry anyway and escape with him to the London conference. Later, she lamented, "How little strong men… appreciate the violence they inflict on the tender sensibilities of a woman's heart, in trying to subjugate her to their will." She likened it to "downright tyranny."[10]

When a woman married in 1840, she became subordinate to her husband. She had no rights to property or to her earnings, could not sign contracts, initiate suits, or establish credit, and could not acquire custody of her own children. Although she knew all of this, it must have distressed Elizabeth. She had excised the word "obey" from her marriage vows, because hers was supposed to be an equitable relationship. After the marriage ceremony on May 1 they spent two days in Peterboro with the Smiths.

In planning the visit, Henry quipped to Gerrit, "We may come in chains—... we shall totally dissent from any proposition of emancipation, immediate or gradual...." On May 10, he told Gerrit, "You know I need not say one word in praise of my newly acquired treasure.... Words cannot express to you my estimate of its value...." Obviously, his opinion of the marriage relationship buried Elizabeth's personhood. She must have been appalled at his reference to her as "it," and as a thing of "value." And she would deal with his conservative possessiveness for the rest of her life.[11]

During their marriage, Henry was away from home for as much as ten months per year on business and political tours, but Elizabeth did not seem to mind. She enjoyed the decision-making autonomy and ran her home and reared her children in accordance with her principles of freedom from male domination. She enjoyed a bright and open house, and, at Seneca Falls, often had new windows and doors installed. Henry once "complained that his epitaph would read 'died of fresh air.'"[12]

When she could get away from home to do her reform work, she developed a unique personal style of operation. As a major philosopher for the women's rights movement, she encouraged autonomy, challenging each woman to become self-reliant. She liked moralizing to the public as a prophet, and saw herself as an agitator for change. She once told Gerrit Smith that through her public appearances, she had been "stirring up women generally to rebellion." Her frankness about oppression often bothered others.

Her reply:

"I would not take back one brave word or deed….
The desire to please those we admire and respect often
cripples conscience." She told a friend in England, "I
feel it to be my special mission to tell people what they
are not prepared to hear, instead of echoing worn-out
opinions."[13]

As a speaker, Cady Stanton was powerful and eloquent with
good wit. Her biographer noted that "She was perceived as mater-
nal, dignified, and eminently respectable." Her radical and opin-
ionated presentations were usually persuasive as she compared the
status of women to that of slaves.[14]

Like Gerrit Smith, Cady Stanton was a practical thinker, and
aimed to reform existing institutions rather than drop out of society to form a perfect order. She believed that creating a network
of individuals and groups would establish the power base needed
for change. She captured the attention and loyalty of others by
attempting to "mitigate" their misery. Lucretia Mott echoed the
sentiments of many when she expressed her "great faith in Elizabeth Stanton's quick instincts + clear insight in all appertaining
to women's rights."[15]

One such insight involved the labels by which women identified themselves. When Boston abolitionist Wendell Phillips
referred to Elizabeth as "Mrs. H. B. Stanton," she replied, "I have
very serious objections… to being called Henry," or being identified as "Mrs." Didn't Phillips know, she asked, "that women +
negroes were beginning to repudiate the name of their masters?"
It made her feel like a chattel slave whose name reflected the
dominance of his owner.

Even cousin Gerrit Smith did not get it. When he addressed
her as "E.C. Stanton," she critically shot back,

"E.C. is no name. Suppose I should write to you Mr. G.S. Fitzhugh. You see my dear cousin you have not taken in the whole idea of woman's degradation."[16]

Her point was that even sophisticated, liberal males could not feel what women felt. "Having denied our identity with himself, he has no data to go upon in judging of our wants and interests." She made that point to the New York State legislature on February 18, 1860, noting that the label "Mrs." conveys possession to the male, and prejudice against women. In fact, she noted, the prejudice in American culture against women was more intense than that against skin color.[17]

But even Cady Stanton had difficulty completely escaping those cultural biases. In her "History of Woman Suffrage," she and her co-editors consistently referred to "Mrs. Gage, Mrs. Davis, Mrs. Lucy Stone, Mrs. Stanton," and others. And in her autobiography she wrote of "Mrs. Horace Smith, Mrs. Baldwin," and "Mrs. Stanton Blatch"—her daughter.[18]

Even though Cady Stanton did not live to see the implementation of many of the reforms she advocated, she was certainly successful in bringing the oppression of women to the attention of the American public. Yet her New York Times obituary noted that she "sought to become an actual political factor by entering the lists for Congress." She would be insulted to know that it was the position of this leading journal that the only way one could become a "political factor" was to run for Congress.[19]

The other major figure in this book is Gerrit Smith.[20] Like his cousin, Smith was born into privilege, his father being of Dutch heritage and his mother a Livingston. Gerrit's father, Peter, was an early partner of John Jacob Astor in the upstate New York fur trade with Native Americans. He became wealthy after investing his profits in land. He became the first judge in Madison County, and both the township of Smithfield and the hamlet of Peterboro bear his name.

Gerrit Smith was schooled in Peterboro before attending Hamilton College in Clinton, New York, graduating in 1818. Because of the death of his mother in 1818 and the retirement of his father in 1819, Gerrit Smith took over the land sales business. He eventually became, in our terms, a philanthropic multi-billionaire, giving away during his lifetime our equivalent of nearly a billion dollars to the causes of oppressed people.

The antislavery and women's rights movements were both recipients of his financial gifts, but most of his donations went to local causes or to individuals in need, thereby rendering him a somewhat invisible leader in American history.

His liberal ideas concerning human rights and religion led him toward causes that would liberate the human mind and body from any type of oppression, and his practical style of thought made him flexible enough to change both himself and his tactics when necessary to achieve a goal. For instance, in the decades of 1830-1860, when the tools being used to pursue the abolition of slavery were not working, he would change tools. He first supported moral suasion, then politics, then violence. Critics of his alleged vacillation miss the point of his adaptability.

In Peterboro, he ran a successful underground railroad station, aiding hundreds of former slaves in their journeys to freedom in Canada. Harriet Tubman, Frederick Douglass, and Jermain Wesley Loguen were his colleagues—often in Peterboro—in that endeavor. His land purchase/sales business occupied most of his time (thirteen hours a day for fifty-five years) and produced the money for his philanthropy. The financial support for John Brown's activities in Kansas and at Harpers Ferry, <u>Frederick Douglass' Paper</u>, and of Harriet Tubman's trips into the South to liberate slaves all came from his micro-managerial work in his small—and extant—Land Office at the west end of the Peterboro Green.

Despite his opposition to being a politician, he was nominated by third parties for president of the United States four times, and for governor of the State of New York three times. The only office he ever held was as a representative of his central New York district to the United States House of Representatives in 1853-1854, and because of his apolitical stance, he served as an independent.

His work for human rights never faltered, although as we shall see, his full commitment to women's rights wavered at one point.

In the context of this book, Gerrit Smith and Elizabeth Cady Stanton were "related" in many ways. As cousins, they knew each other intimately. As colleagues, they worked toward similar goals. As mutual critics, they kept each other aware of their own faults and inconsistencies. And as friends, their mutual support was unwavering.

TWO

The Issues

"These… discussions at my cousin's fireside I count among the great blessings of my life."
—Elizabeth Cady Stanton, late in her life

The Peterboro home and family of Gerrit Smith had such a strong influence on the young Elizabeth Cady that she remembered them in later years as a "blessing." Her extended summer visits there started when she was a girl; she remembered "wading in a modest stream that… creeps slowly round the grounds." One biographer of Elizabeth referred to her younger days as those of "a carefree tomboy…."

Living in Johnstown, NY as a young girl, she graduated from Johnstown Academy in 1830. Next at Emma Willard's Female Seminary she was taught to appreciate broad interests, learning self-confidence and assertiveness. After graduating from Troy Seminary in 1833, Elizabeth often visited relatives, and "for solace she turned to her relatives in Peterboro." Although there was an 18-year difference in the ages of the two cousins, they considered themselves to be colleagues in the reform movements as early as the 1830s.[1]

By that time, the Smiths had renounced the strict and conservative Calvinism of their past and enjoyed liberal thought, play, humor and games. One of the reasons that Elizabeth Cady enjoyed visits to Peterboro was the presence there of another (second) cousin—Gerrit and Ann Smith's daughter Elizabeth

Smith, born September 20, 1822. The two young girls became close friends and enjoyed "all kinds of games, and practical jokes carried beyond all bounds of propriety."

Later they became colleagues in the women's rights movement for over fifty years, with Cady making regular visits to Peterboro and, later, to Elizabeth Smith Miller's home in Geneva. "The year with us," Cady said, "was never considered complete without a visit to Peterboro…." She loved the hospitality practiced there: "Their warm sympathies and sweet simplicity of manner melted the sternest natures and made the most reserved amiable." She called Peterboro a "green spot" and a "peaceful abode" in her life, and craved the cultural diversity that existed there.[2]

The Smith home was a Mecca for reformers whose work spanned many issues. In the 1830s, Elizabeth Cady said of it,

> "Here one would meet the first families in the State, with Indians, Africans, slaveholders, religionists of all sects, and representatives of all shades of humanity, each class alike welcomed and honored, feasting, fêting, dancing—joining in all kinds of amusements and religious worship together…."

Gerrit Smith's friend and early biographer noted:

> "I have seen eating in peace, at one time, at dinner, in his house—all welcome guests—an Irish Catholic priest, a Hicksite Quakeress minister, a Calvinistic Presbyterian deacon of the Jonathan Edwards school, two abolition lecturers, a seventh-day Baptist, a shouting Methodist, a Whig pro-slavery member of Congress, a Democratic official of the 'Sam Young school,' a southern ex-slave holder and a runaway slave, Lewis Washington by name, also his wife, one or more

relatives, and "Aunt Betsy' Kelty. And he managed them all. Not one was neglected."³

One early influence on Elizabeth Cady's liberal ideas regarding women's rights came through her acquaintance in Peterboro with Native Americans of the Oneida Nation. Their social structure was matriarchal, with women making all of the major social, political and economic decisions. This contrasted with what she saw around her, and she began to wonder why women in her culture had so little power.

She also had her human rights concerns stimulated by the issue of the abolition of slavery. At the Smith home she would meet such abolitionists as Frederick Douglass, William Lloyd Garrison, Wendell Phillips, Beriah Green, Stephen and Abbey Kelley Foster, John Brown, Franklin B. Sanborn, George Thompson, and Charles Stuart. "It was with such company," she said, "that I spent weeks every year…. These rousing arguments at Peterboro made social life seem tame and profitless elsewhere."⁴

She later recalled,

> "…One time, when Frederick Douglass came to spend a few days at Peterboro,… [we] walked about with him, arm in arm, played games, and sang songs together. He playing the accompaniment on the guitar."

Certainly "games" were not their only concern. Douglass was one of the most powerful, radical and eloquent abolitionists in the country, and he would not have made a trip to Peterboro just to sing. Her brother-in-law Edward Bayard

> "argued all the time [with Gerrit] upon the subject of abolition. I enjoyed it very much as they both argue well and without the least impatience either in word or manner."⁵

The year 1839 was an important one for Cady's Peterboro connection. She attended what she would later describe as,

> "a series of anti-slavery conventions… being held in Madison County…. I felt a new inspiration in life and was enthused with new ideas of individual rights…."

It was in that year that a slave woman named Harriet Powell escaped from her owner while on a trip to Syracuse, and was brought to the Smith home for protection and for transportation to Canada. While she was at Peterboro, Gerrit said,

> "Harriet, I have brought all my young cousins to see you. I want you to make good abolitionists of them by telling them the history of your life—what you have seen and suffered in slavery."

Elizabeth Cady responded, "we needed no further education to make us earnest abolitionists." Eighteen hours later, after Harriet had been transported north, her owner appeared in Peterboro to claim his property. Gerrit had him stay for dinner.[6]

In October 1839, Elizabeth Cady met Henry Brewster Stanton in Peterboro. While on a central New York tour as a speaker at antislavery meetings, abolitionist Stanton had stopped at Peterboro for a visit with the Smiths. After a short and controversial courtship, they married on May 1, 1840 and promptly sailed to the World Antislavery Convention in London. In sum, Elizabeth wrote to Ann Smith,

> "I cannot tell you dear cousin with how much pleasure, + how often, in memory I go back + enjoy again the many weeks I spent with you…. I shall never forget those happy days…."[7]

During her later life, Cady Stanton maintained the highly valued contact with the Smith family. After her 1862 move to the New York City area, she made "annual pilgrimages to… Peterboro…." Throughout the 1880s and 1890s she spent several weeks during most summers at Elizabeth Smith Miller's lakeside home in Geneva. "She and I have been most faithful, devoted friends all our lives," said Cady Stanton, "and regular correspondents for more than fifty years."[8]

The two main persons who are the subjects of this book—Elizabeth Cady Stanton and Gerrit Smith—both possessed an extraordinarily high level of self-confidence and a lack of fear of the personal consequences of speaking and acting on behalf of the oppressed. They felt the urgent need to agitate and advocate, and they expended little effort seeking public approval. Both excelled at using the mind to analyze a problem and pursue solutions, and each felt exhilaration over the possibility of fueling social change toward equality among people.

Their work demanded self-denial and sacrifice with intense focus. As one of their abolitionist colleagues put it, "Self-indulgence will have no fellowship with our stern… fanaticism."[9]

As they worked at human rights issues through the decades, their political thought varied. As practical thinkers they could survey the contingencies around them, note the practical requirements of the moment, and adjust their strategies and tactics to maximize the potential for success.

This makes categorization of their efforts difficult; at different times they could be liberal, conservative, or radical. In the eyes of some critics, these inconsistencies led to charges of weakness. But in this author's view, it led to their becoming the most powerful and influential persons in both movements: Smith in the abolition movement, and Cady Stanton in the women's rights movement.

As Sue Davis put it in "The Practical Thought of Elizabeth Cady Stanton,"

> "...the presence of inconsistencies in an individual's political thought should not be taken as an indication of weakness in her or his work.... Ideas are invariably connected to the circumstances in which they are formulated... [and] are... inevitably intertwined with goals and strategies."

Indeed! The ability to "shift gears," to "punt," and to choose a different strategy is akin to choosing a better tool to accomplish a task. It is the maintenance of consistency above all things that leads to weakness, not the ability to adapt.[10]

Smith and Cady Stanton were perceptive enough of social conditions to figure out what was possible in the short term as they pursued the seemingly impossible in the long term. They sought out new ideas and techniques to deal with conflicted people—including themselves—and agreed that the only consistency in complex human behavior is inconsistency.

Their work in New York State amounted to a rallying cry for the nation. In fact, New York State was at the center of the reform movements—both abolition and women's rights. Cady Stanton wrote, "A full report of the woman's rights agitation in the State of New York, would in a measure be the history of the movement." And, as a challenging idea, consider this: If New York State could have been isolated from the rest of the United States during the three decades before 1860, there might not have been a Civil War. That is how radical and powerful the abolitionists there were.[11]

Both Stanton and Smith must have been inspiring people to know. Even getting to "know" them *now* is inspiring. They were healthy   physically and mentally, profound thinkers and passionate activists, well-educated and highly literate, witty (Cady Stanton more than Smith), expert at exposing oppression, and exemplary in knowing what to do about it.

Cady Stanton's opinion of Smith was very positive. She admired how he stuck to principle in the face of opposition. In one reference to him she claimed,

> "If the success of our cause could be assured by the high character of the men who from the beginning have identified… with it, woman would have been emancipated long ago."

When Smith's grandson Gerrit Smith Miller was born, Cady Stanton wished that he "may be just such another fanatic as he is whose name you bear…." And when Gerrit's actions needed guidance, she felt free to give it when she wrote to Ann,

> "I sent [cousin Gerrit] a little [advice] in a former letter, but as he is so self-willed, it probably had no effect. Now we wish you to make him mind."[12]

Elizabeth's opinion of most men was not very high or positive. She wished that

> "every young man… would devote his talents to the best interests of the race, rather than to his personal ambition for mere worldly success."

What she admired about Smith was his ability to use his own life as an example of what should *not* be, and to employ philanthropy optimistically to foster change. But for Smith—as we shall see later regarding woman suffrage—donating money was a lot easier than adjusting his ideas. Although he may have wavered in his support for suffrage, his support—at least in principle—for women's rights was solid.

Frederick Douglass commented about Smith specifically, and about Cady Stanton by implication,

> "It is not alone because of the goodness of any cause that [we] can safely predicate success. Much depends on the character and quality of the men and women who are its advocates.... Only the best of mankind can afford to support unpopular opinions. The common sort will drift with the tide."[13]

Certainly Cady Stanton and Smith were not "the common sort." They realized both the seriousness and the difficulty of their endeavors; they were not so naïve as to think that writing new laws would quickly change the status of slaves and women. They knew that people would have to change their values about equality before real equality could be achieved. And they committed their lives to the reform process toward that end.

THREE

The Reform Era

"[There was a] brilliant circle of Boston transcendentalists, who hoped in a few years to transform our selfish, competitive civilization into a Paradise where all altruistic values might make cooperation possible."
—Elizabeth Cady Stanton[1]

Optimism exploded in the 1820s like a brilliant burst of fireworks. It grew out of what came to be called the Second Great Awakening—a revival of religion that swept through the northeastern states like a fire storm. That decade saw the death of the old Calvinism that emphasized the power of authority and submission to fate. New "transcendentalist" thought emerged. The new direction emphasized the importance of the individual and the human capacity for achievement. Self-reliance, hard work and persistence, coupled with moral responsibility, fueled optimism that one could improve his own position and, through philanthropy, help society to develop more equitable treatment for all people.

With the chains of authoritarian paternalism removed, human-rights movements became secular expressions of this new attitude. Some people 'dropped out' and formed isolated experiments in 'perfectionism' like the Oneida Community in central

New York. Others dug in and attempted to reform the existing social system from the inside. Young, well-educated people with active and creative minds, who could *feel* the pains of discrimination, ushered in social movements with the help of like-minded friends. Elizabeth Cady Stanton and Gerrit Smith were two such people, and moral agitation became their technique for rousing and mobilizing the public conscience.

Throughout the 1820s, reform societies multiplied in religious and temperance circles, and women were some of their major players. It's fair to say that the changes in popular thinking initiated by the Second Great Awakening led to the antislavery movement in the early 1830s, which in turn encouraged the development of the women's rights movement in the early 1840s. And the initial optimism of both the abolitionists and the women's rights supporters was justified by the success that organizers of the Second Great Awakening had in changing the moral quality of the lives of many people. By 1835, revivalism had inspired reformers to believe that a glorious new era of righteousness, peace, and equality was at hand. The evangelistic crusade had succeeded in developing some enlightened people who opposed oppression, cruelty, and injustice.

But the abolitionists and women's rights advocates may not have realized that the changes from the Second Great Awakening came as a matter of individual choice, whereas the reforms sought by these two human rights movements would require fundamental changes in the values of an entire society.

The Reform Era was a complex drama on an epic scale. It emerged from the contradiction between glorious Revolutionary Era ideals about personal liberty and the effort to implement those ideals amidst the realities of slavery and the oppression of women. One of the greatest ironies in this context was that whereas there were some cases of collaboration between blacks and whites,[2] similar alliances between men and women were rare, and even the seemingly solid ones—such as Smith and Cady Stanton, or Douglass and Cady Stanton—fell apart over the issue of suffrage.

Women and blacks wanted not just a patched-up legal system which would allow them freedom or the vote, but a reformed social system that would guarantee equality.

As the 1820s gave way to the 1830s, the new optimism coupled with a "market revolution" that would change how people could live. The world was changing from isolated agricultural families to a manufacturing-based economy that linked many communities. New advances in communications, transportation, urbanization, trade, technologies, and even political options produced a type of nineteenth-century "future shock." People struggled with new social patterns and values that raised perplexing questions and begged for change: Was slavery right? Were women to be counted as citizens? Were Native Americans savages? Were poor people equals?

In such a context, individual rights became prominent as social horizons expanded and people felt optimistic about change. Expectations soared and confronted established power relationships, igniting the dynamics of social movements. As old worlds shattered, people struggled to link the mosaic of new ideas, behaviors, expectations and roles. Balance—both personal and across communities—was elusive. People who were threatened by the rush of new ideas sought refuge in religion or in alcohol. New competitive, capitalistic values challenged people's visions of a utopian community from one of stability to one of opportunity. And in the midst of it all, the new realities spawned reformers.

The basic premise of both the antislavery movement and the women's rights movement was "the essential injustice of human bondage," whether on the plantation or in the home. An international trend of recognizing human rights had lagged in the United

States, and budding reformers were determined to bring that fact to public attention. As the 1830s dawned, they saw a dichotomy of social trends: collective moral change to secure human rights competed with individual debauchery that squandered social stability. Whereas the latter trend used the 'new-era' emphasis on the individual for personal and selfish gains, the reformers sought to use it for the benefit of individuals who were oppressed.

Reformers were usually young people who were challenging the establishment. They felt aggrieved by public indifference to those who were oppressed, and they understood that there is no such thing as a little bit of freedom. With the new cultural emphasis on empowering the individual, they saw slow, gradual improvement as a recipe for revolt, and demanded more immediate equality. Their intense focus and boundless energy earned them the label of fanatics—which they took as a compliment. As abolition researcher Bertram Wyatt-Brown put it, reformers were those "whose compulsive dissatisfaction with prevailing mores is antithetical to the ordinary process of slow improvement."[3]

The reformer was generally not an intellectual or a politician who weighed all aspects of a situation and sought compromise; his or her strategy rested in the assertion of moral principles instead of in social or political skills. Therefore, their power came from their ability to impress the public audience. And in the instances when that did not happen, they looked pathetic.

The two major players in this book—Cady Stanton and Smith—fit this description of a reformer quite well. They both rejected the status quo, and they agreed with their contemporary philosopher Henry David Thoreau that the reason reform activity was necessary was because people had consciences. For them, the influence of conscience overrode the power of the state and tradition. The traditional idea was that good citizenship meant conformity. The new idea was that individual conscience and civil disobedience were the backbone of a principled, democratic government. The 'Higher Law' of moral conscience should prevail over civil law.

As reformers, they knew that radical change was needed in the social fabric, not just a change in the laws. They were convinced of their goals and determined to persist, no matter what the consequences might be. As Cady Stanton biographer Elizabeth Griffith put it,

> "Cautious, careful people… never can bring about a reform. Those who are really in earnest must be willing to be anything or nothing in the world's estimation, and… avow their sympathy with despised and persecuted ideas and [people], and bear the consequences."[4]

Cady Stanton was grateful that she lived at a time when reform was possible, when change and progress were stimulated by new ideas. Like Smith, she accepted the need for systemic rather than partial reform. As Cady Stanton said,

> "Let us remember that all reforms are interdependent and that whatever is done to establish one principle on a solid basis strengthens all. Reformers who are [willing to compromise] have not yet grasped [this] idea…. The object… is not to carry one fragmentary measure in human progress…."

They also agreed that the process had to start with the reformer setting the initial example, then attempting to spread that model to one's home, then to one's local community, the county, the state, and the nation. "Radical reform," Cady Stanton said, "must start in our homes, in our nurseries, in ourselves." Their effort was to challenge what they saw as moral depravity through example.[5]

That example was designed to mitigate the "vicious circle" of discrimination; that is, those who are discriminated against become poor, and the poverty is used as a justification of discrimination, which leads to more poverty, and so on. As early antislavery advocate Richard Allen put it,

> "Will you plead our incapacity for freedom, and our contented condition under oppression, as a sufficient cause for keeping us under the previous yoke?"[6]

The yoke was heavy on the shoulders of Elizabeth Cady Stanton, who became the main philosopher of the women's rights movement. Her ideas challenged the status quo of male dominance that had excluded women from most spheres of public life. She illuminated the sources of discrimination and suggested possible solutions, realizing that the fight against the intense bias of sexism would be difficult. She wrote,

> "To grant woman an equality with man in the affairs of life is contrary to every tradition, every precedent, every inheritance, every instinct and every teaching."

And she noted the effect of this on women:

> "They are more conservative even than men, because of the narrowness and isolation of their lives, the subjection in which they always have been held, the severe punishment inflicted by society on those who dare step outside the prescribed sphere, and, stronger than all, perhaps, their religious tendencies through which it has been impressed upon them that their subordinate position was assigned by the Divine will and that to rebel against it is to defy the Creator. In all the generations, Church, State and society have combined to retard the development of women…."

She remarked that women had withstood such legal "oppression with… stupid fortitude… for six thousand years."[7]

One avenue of potential change that held promise for the followers of both abolition and women's rights was the rapid advancement of science in the decades before the Civil War. New knowledge in both mechanical and social sciences made life more understandable, predictable, and controllable. The optimistic reformers believed that this could help them develop institutions appropriate to the elimination of selfishness and the advancement of a more harmonious society. They argued that data received by the senses should guide decisions more than tradition and superstition. Cady Stanton saw "Women of all classes… awakening to the necessity of self-support," and she expressed the hope that science applied to daily life would aid that process.[8]

However optimistic this sounds, it was improbable that new data would be able to dissolve male insensitivity to women, or whites' insensitivity to blacks. In both of these cases, empathy failed; it seems that Cady Stanton could not conceive of herself as black, and Smith could not conceive of himself as a woman. This is ironic in that both of them believed in the principle of "self-application" to test the legitimacy of any position. That is, follow the Golden Rule, and do not treat any person in a way that you would not want to be treated.

Here, I will use the case of Smith's inability to conceive of himself as a woman as an example of a quality of human relationships that leads to social movements. As Cady Stanton said in general terms, "it is impossible for the best of men to understand women's feelings or the humiliation of their position." Even Gerrit Smith, a champion of human rights, had difficulty identifying with women, and he only exemplified in elite fashion the insensitivity of most males of that era.[9]

When Smith opposed divorce, referred to Cady Stanton as "Mrs.," and refused to support woman suffrage, he received the following response from her:

> "Well now, suppose yourself as a woman. You are educated up to that point where one feels a deep interest in the welfare of her country, and in all the great questions of the day, in both Church and State; yet you have no voice in either.... How much complacency... would [you] feel in your womanhood?
>
> "Judge by yourself then, how long the women of this nation will consent to be deprived of their social, civil and political rights...."

Smith had said that, in all cases except for the biological functions of reproduction, men and women were alike. Stanton countered,

> "If you truly believe that man is woman, and woman is man; if you believe that all the burning indignation that fires your soul at the sight of injustice and oppression would nerve you to a life-long struggle for liberty and independence, then know that what you feel, I feel too, and what I feel the mass of women feel also."[10]

But she was skeptical of his claims, and was actually chastising her cousin for his hypocrisy. "A privileged class," she said, "can never conceive the feelings of those who are born to contempt, to inferiority, to degradation." Feeling that degradation intensely in her own life, she complained that the human rights oratory of women "could not hurt him, entrenched, as he is behind creeds, codes, customs, and constitutions, with vizor and breastplate of self-complacency and conceit."

She even cracked her oratorical whip at the male attendees at a gathering of the American Anti-Slavery Society:

> "To you, white man, the world throws wide her gates; the way is clear to wealth, to fame, to glory, to renown; the high places of independence and honor and trust are yours; all your efforts are praised and encouraged, all your successes are welcomed with loud hurrahs and cheers; but the black man and the woman are born to shame."[11]

The pain and indignation felt by Cady Stanton and the millions of women she so ably represented were intensified by the traditional expectations that became recognized as masculine and feminine gender roles.

FOUR

Sex, Gender, and Social Roles

"Well-behaved women seldom make history."
—Laurel Thatcher Ulrich, 1976

Historian Laurel Ulrich penned this "ambiguous wisdom" in 1976, and it became a slogan for the expanding feminist movement of the day. Cady Stanton would certainly have agreed. The reason that the slogan works in favor of women's rights, Ulrich wrote, is "it plays into longstanding stereotypes about the invisibility… of the female sex."[1]

Sex is a biological concept that refers to the physiological differences between males and females. It is ascribed at conception and is not influenced by culture-based or learned factors. Gender, however, is a cultural concept that refers to differences in feminine and masculine roles.

The difference in the definition of these two concepts is of monumental importance. Confusing them, or equating them—as is often done in popular or journalistic circles—obscures the meaning of what one says or writes. When we mention "sex," we refer directly to males or females. When we mention "gender," we refer to any person who displays masculine or feminine traits or roles as defined by the relevant culture. Such roles vary among cultures due to varying local emphasis on what are considered to be proper roles for each gender. According to sociologists, "Gender is a basic organizing principle of society that shapes how we think... and guides how we interact with others... [And] it involves <u>hierarchy</u>, because it affects the opportunities and constraints we face throughout our lives."[2]

Although sex is inherited, gender is not. The huge fallacy of thought comes when we assume that gender roles are immutable, or that they can be assigned in rigid fashion to either sex. When English philosopher Herbert Spencer's idea of "social Darwinism" first appeared in print in 1850, it noted that the struggle among various social elements was a natural process that was inevitable, beneficial, and led toward balance. This was a conservative ideology that justified inequality. People—men and women—with supposedly immutable behavioral traits arranged themselves in superior and inferior positions. Through this belief, dominance becomes normal and legitimate, while reform appears to be the impossible dream of foolish minds.

Because we know that gender identity is not assignable by sex, and is always in flux, an interesting question is, when is gender identity established in the development of a person? Recent research completed by urologist Sidney W. Ecker offers some insight.

A continuum exists regarding the distribution of the intensity of masculine/feminine traits and thoughts:

Masculine   **Feminine**

Some people are very masculine and some are very feminine, while the majority share a mix of both types. Both are present in every person, and any one person—male or female—may be overbalanced in either direction. The dominant direction—masculine or feminine—is determined early in fetal development *before* gonads and hormones are developed. The factor that determines this is the number of neurons available as protein receptors in the brain to receive the hormones eventually produced by the gonads. The masculine and feminine hormone receptors in the brain exist before the gonads and hormones can influence them. Therefore, the dominance of either determines one's gender identity before the existence of physical sexual identity.

The startling conclusion of this research is that

> "... gender identity cannot be predicted from anatomy…. One cannot deny the profound effects of Testosterone, Estradiol and other steroids on genital differentiation… but gender identity is determined before and persists in spite of these effects."[3]

Given this information, it is ludicrous to claim that either sex—male or female, as physically identified—could possess any 'proper' list of masculine or feminine traits. And the same can probably be said for any 'race', whatever that word means.

In the pre-Civil-War Reform Era, as the mega-forces of industrialization, urbanization, and an explosion in communications technology changed the socio-economic terrain of American culture, gender became a tool for classifying and ordering a population in flux. Claims of racial or gender purity or superiority were constructed by those in charge as defensive tactics against their perceived enemies. Actually, such purity or exclusivity is impossible when people are properly perceived as gender hybrids. All human identities are in flux, and the refusal to see this requires bias to sustain it. By not implementing the bias, 'merged-identity' people threaten the dominance of others by weakening the certainties of those differences in sex and gender they have wrongly claimed, and thereby reducing the power inherent in this false system of dichotomies.

To maintain their position of superiority and social dominance established over thousands of years prior to the reform era, white males needed to construct a bastion of defense. They assigned to women a cluster of supposedly feminine traits that were designed to keep them subservient. Their success at this reflected society's longstanding negative attitude toward women.

Sally Kitch, a professor of Women and Gender Studies at Arizona State University, has noted in her research that previous to our Civil War, men assumed that

> "The 'natural' gender order, mandated by woman's
> irrationality, passions, and God-ordained dependence,
> required female confinement to the domestic sphere
> and submission to male control over their property,
> persons, and prospects."

This attitude resulted in the male belief that women should be controlled for their own good. Although women's labor in a home was seen as useful in balancing assigned tasks, women were still insulted; such a patronizing attitude made equality a utilitarian notion.[4]

The main social value of women was their moral influence on male-dominated homes and communities. Women supposedly lacked practical reasoning powers and were weak, delicate, and emotional compared to the stronger, more intelligent men. Even pro-women's rights abolitionist William Lloyd Garrison wrote,

> "Nature has provided opposite spheres for the two
> sexes, and neither can pass over the limits of the other
> without deviating from the... decorum of their respec-
> tive characters."[5]

Elizabeth Cady Stanton lamented this attitude:

> "Men… are so thoroughly educated into the belief that woman's nature is altogether different from their own, that they have no idea that she can be governed by the same laws of mind as themselves. So far from viewing us like themselves, they seem… to consider us their moral and intellectual [opposites]…."[6]

This nineteenth-century bias that favored men for political roles influenced even the most liberal-minded people. Gerrit Smith believed that human rights were universal, but he also thought that women were not strong enough to carry their movement to success. With 'genderist' thought typical of the period, he believed that femininity dulled one's mind and ambition. Such thoughts led men either to think negatively about women, or to ignore them altogether.

The wording of the United States Constitution ignores women completely: every sex-specific pronoun in it refers to men. In a personal case, when Elizabeth Cady's only brother died just after having graduated from college, her grief-stricken father Daniel said to her, "Oh, my daughter, I wish you were a boy." What's more, both then and now, the tradition of the father "giving away" the bride is a symptom of women being owned and controlled by men.[7]

The supposed weakness of the female extended to her full responsibility for 'sins' that were equally attributable to men, such as prostitution. Abolitionist Arthur Tappan initiated an effort in New York City to reform those "females who have deviated from the path of virtue."

Public advertising also emphasized female weakness. Hops and Malt Bitters were "especially recommended for all the various Complaints and Diseases of Women, such as Mental Depression,

Weakness, Breaking Down, Lassitude of the System, Headache, Dizziness, etc."

And Ryer's Sarsaparilla was recommended for the one-half of American women who were not of "sound health. They are disordered, and their condition is leaving its imprint on the rising generation. [Their disorder is caused by] a want of constitutional strength...."

With all these negative ideas and feelings about women, it is not surprising that the 'proper' roles assigned to them put them in a social position that limited their power—and was not the least bit threatening to men.[8]

The nineteenth-century stereotype of the proper woman placed her solely in the domestic sphere; differences between men and women were considered to be natural, inherited, immutable, and deterministic. Women were quiet, delicate, intuitive, religious, subservient, sensitive, emotional, moral, and of course, idle. These traits were reinforced by contemporary social customs, the Judeo-Christian tradition, patriarchal institutions, English common law, and American statutes. As moral beings, a major responsibility of women was the taming of the natural competitiveness and aggression of men.

These traits also made women the most appropriate child-rearers. Cady Stanton observed that when a mother died, the children were "scattered to the four winds of heaven" because the father could not or would not care for them. In fact, when abolitionist and Liberty Party presidential nominee James G. Birney's wife (Gerrit Smith's sister-in-law) died, his children spent years being reared by Smith's family in Peterboro.[9]

This domestic image of the ideal woman who put everyone else's needs above her own in order to keep a happy household was despised by Cady Stanton, who believed that the image had to be "killed" in self-defense.

A stereotype also existed for the male. He was assumed to be strong, courageous and invulnerable. His practical thought led to decisiveness, and his mechanical skills encouraged a self-assuredness that could be oppressive. As Cady Stanton saw it,

> "Men… are fond of representing themselves as beings of reason—of intellect—while women are mere creatures of the affections. There is a self conceit that makes the possessor [unlikely] to dispel the illusion."

They are "so absorbed in outward improvements + material gains that the everlasting principles of right have been lost sight of, buried as they are beneath heaps of gold dust and cotton."[10]

She saw the "male element" as

> "… a destructive force, stern, selfish, aggrandizing, loving war, violence, conquest, acquisition, breeding in the material and moral world alike discord, disorder, disease, and death. [While men have ruled], see what… slavery, slaughter,… inquisitions and imprisonments, pains and persecutions, black codes and gloomy creeds, the seed of humanity have struggled with for the centuries while mercy has veiled her face…."[11]

Men, she thought, were so vain and insensitive that they feigned concern over the moral purity of women as a means of covering their own hypocrisy. They seemed to understand little of the complexity of a woman's life. She wrote,

> "Men who can, when they wish to write a document, shut themselves up for days with their thoughts and their books, know little of what difficulties a woman must surmount to get off a tolerable production."

She used as an example an experience she had at a convention in Ann Arbor, Michigan in November of 1869:

> "One gentleman had the moral hardihood to assert that men had more endurance than women, whereupon a lady remarked that she would like to see... young men... laced up in steel-ribbed corsets, with hoops, heavy skirts, trains, high heels, panniers, chignons, and dozens of hairpins sticking in their scalps, cooped up in the house year after year, with no exhilarating exercise, no hopes, aims, nor ambitions in life and know if they could stand it as well as the girls."[12]

Women who were beginning to question their static roles viewed these male attitudes as oppressive. Men, however, claimed that women's roles and male attitudes were justified by God. Their evidence was the The Bible: Genesis 3:16 gave to the husband the power to "rule over" women, and Ephesians 5:22-23 required women to "submit" to their husbands.

By the 1830s, some brave women were making noise about the discrimination they faced. Sarah and Angelina Grimké were sisters from a South Carolina slave-holding family. Together, they disavowed slavery and moved to Philadelphia, where they shocked a conservative public by writing and speaking as abolitionists. Angelina—called "Devilina" by proslavery people—was the first woman to speak about abolition before a state legislature. Her speaking tour of New England was supported by the recently formed American Anti-Slavery Society. On February 21, 1838 she famously told the Massachusetts state legislators, "We abolition women are turning the world upside down."[13]

Earlier, in 1837, Sarah had written,

> "Oh! How many of my sex feel in the dominion... unrighteously exercised over them, under the gentle

appellation of <u>protection</u>, that what they have leaned upon has proved [to be] a broken reed at best, and oft a spear."

She might have approved of our contemporary comment that "any woman searching for a husband has not had one." Sarah also noted,

> "Woman… has been regarded as the slave, or the play thing of man, a being <u>created for him</u>, created mainly to minister to his material comfort, to surrender herself to the gratification of his passions and appetites… willing to live on his earnings, and recline in his bowers."[14]

The metaphor of women as slaves was extreme, but illustrative. Cady Stanton often used it, noting that, as slaves said, they felt mistreated and abused not because they were punished, but because they were *slaves*. The accepted image of white women at the time was that they were privileged and pampered lovers of wonderful males. But Sarah Grimké, writing of the "lust of dominion" that plagued men, said, "All I ask of our brethren is, that they will take their feet… off our necks and permit us to stand upright…."[15]

Cady Stanton saw the attempts by men to keep women out of public roles as based in a prejudice "very like that prejudice against color…." The result was a domestic form of tyranny: "Man [has] exercised a tyranny over her injurious to himself and benumbing to <u>her</u> faculties…." Women, she said, lived in "ignorance" and made "ladders" out of themselves "by which their husbands, brothers and sons climb up into the kingdom of knowledge…."[16]

The movement that Cady Stanton and the Grimké sisters embarked on was designed to liberate women from the perceived tyranny of prejudice and imposed roles. Cady Stanton knew that,

"When woman does… give to the world a full revelation of her sufferings and miseries—the histories of all
other kinds of injustice and oppression will sink into
utter insignificance before the living pictures she shall
hold up to the unwilling vision of domestic tyrants."

Even in her own family, there was opposition. Her father,
attorney Daniel Cady, chastised her for assuming a public role,
and he threatened to disinherit her. And her husband resented
her assertiveness and opposed her writings.[17]

Her reaction to opposition within her family was succinct:

"What is it to me whether the man who robs me of my
[natural] rights is a father, a brother, a husband, or a
Southern slave-holder? Is my loss less, because the blow
is struck at the hearthstone?... Resistance to tyrants is
obedience to God."

Those "tyrants" could be well-educated men in what she called
"high places," such as pulpits, legislatures, courts, and businesses.
"No rude jest," she claimed, "from an ignorant ruffian could so
stir a proud woman's blood as a well-written travesty on her sex
from the pen of a man of learning and position." One such man
was her "dear Cousin," Gerrit Smith.[18]

Smith was an abolitionist by action and a women's rights man
by voice. But words are cheap. As will be seen more clearly later,
he balked at divorce, would not meet his wife and daughter's financial wishes, and opposed women's suffrage at the time when
it was ripe to be acquired.

But Smith's greatest "tyranny" was his control over his two
sons. Fitzhugh and Greene Smith were both groomed by Gerrit
to represent his aristocratic family and take over his lucrative land
sales business. Neither of them wanted to do it, and in spite of

his wife's warnings to let them be what they wanted to be, Gerrit persisted.

Fitzhugh died unexpectedly at age twelve, leaving his father deeply disappointed and depressed. Greene lived to age thirty-eight, becoming an outdoor enthusiast and an ornithologist. Gerrit was angry with him because he never indicated any interest in business. Cady Stanton's oblique reference to Gerrit reads,

> "Many men who are well known for their philanthropy, who hate oppression on a southern plantation, can play the tyrant right well at home."[19]

The reaction of women to this domestic tyranny was to inaugurate assertive new roles. Because women were reared to be passive domestic servants, activists had to overcome reticence, shyness, opposition to their participating in politics or speaking in public, family hostility, and community opposition to women out of place—and still keep up with the demands of housekeeping and rearing children. In an 1839 letter, Susan B. Anthony wrote,

> "What an absurd notion that women have not intellectual and moral faculties sufficient for anything but domestic concerns."

Cady Stanton noted that women "have awakened," and that

> "Alone they must meet the terrible emergencies of life, to be sustained and protected amid danger and death by their own courage, skill and self-reliance, or perish."

Interestingly, many abolitionists accepted the assertive women and welcomed them into previously all male circles. But by 1840, much of that support had eroded due to the fear that attention to women's rights would dilute the emphasis on blacks' rights.[20]

In an ironic twist, even some of the most assertive women seemed to be mired in old cultural stereotypes, their abstract principles clouded by traditional biases. When the New York State Legislature passed a bill to allow a woman to have a bank account under her sole control, Cady Stanton said, "Let the women of the Empire State return countless thanks to their sires and sons." WHAT?! She groveled on her knees in thanks to men for granting her a right! In accordance with the principle of natural rights, governments can only protect rights—not grant them. And when encouraging women to develop a "modicum of respect and power," she advised that they should model "purity, virtue, [and] morality," the very traits that stereotyped women as being weak.[21]

Cady Stanton told Gerrit's daughter, Elizabeth Smith Miller, that if Gerrit's business clerk Caleb Calkins, whom she had interviewed, had been a woman, she would "have asked him a great many more" questions. This implied that women reveal more "secrets" than men. And when lamenting over the death of John Brown and the sickness of Gerrit Smith, she commented, "In times like these, every one should do the work of a full-grown man." It appears that even the most radical thinkers could not completely escape the influence of cultural bais.[22]

In the abolition movement, those men who met in Philadelphia in December 1833 to organize the American Anti-Slavery Society expected women to form their own such organizations. The few men who did support female participation were called "Miss Nancys," and were considered to be weak and socially impotent.[23]

The response of both sexes to "separate-sphere" exclusivity bias was to seek out same-sex support. Close relationships among persons of the same sex were acceptable in nineteenth-century America. There was little concern over gayness or lesbianism, and because the masculine/feminine spheres were so segregated, same-sex social contacts were the norm in occupations, education, hobbies and entertainment, politics, and most other institutional areas.[24]

Male abolitionists sought and preferred each other's company to that of women. They traveled and roomed together—perhaps for safety, and certainly for mutual support. Cultural proscriptions of female participation in male circles actually encouraged the close relationships within both sexes. There existed a general distrust of women as being capable of leadership. This prejudice was supported strongly by most Christian denominations. Within the same-sex social groups, relationships among men tended to be more emotional while those among women were more functional. Even written correspondences among abolitionists were usually among two men, with one woman occasionally adding a line addressing the other's wife.

It was the "Boston clique" of abolitionists—followers of William Lloyd Garrison—that claimed to accept the participation of women in their organized activities. But that acceptance was largely rhetorical: women were thought to add some moral respectability to the men's act, and to help with fund-raising. The male abolitionists' sincerity about bonding with female colleagues has been questioned on the basis of their usually cool relationships with their wives. Garrison and Wendell Phillips, two major leaders of the Boston group, wondered if they should ever have married, as did Gerrit Smith during his 'mid-life crisis'. So the same-sex relationships for both men and women can be properly seen as supportive group therapy for people who were frequently 'beaten up' by public opinion and actions. They were attempts to maintain personal balance and collective motivation and enthusiasm to continue the crusade for freedom and justice for all.[25]

As radical leaders of the women's rights movement and the abolition movement, Elizabeth Cady Stanton and Gerrit Smith both claimed that full understanding and cooperation between the sexes was their goal, and that the Golden Rule of "self-application" would aid the process of achieving it.

Cady Stanton claimed:

> "When man shall fully grasp the idea that woman is a being of like feelings, thoughts and passions with himself, he may be able to legislate for her, as one code would answer for both."

Smith claimed:

> "What woman needs to believe and man also, is that, with the exception of that physical difference, which is for the multiplication and perpetuation of the race, man is woman, and woman is man."

To Susan B. Anthony he wrote,

> "There is but one standard of modesty and delicacy for both men and women…. It is my duty to be as modest and delicate as you are…."[26]

Such ideas of gender convergence were rare, and they generally fell upon deaf ears at both the public and legislative levels. In addressing the New York State Legislature, Cady Stanton observed,

> "When we plead our cause before the law-makers and servants of the republic, they can not take in the idea that men and women are alike; and so long as the mass rest in this delusion, the public mind will not be so much startled by the revelations made of the injustice and degradation of woman's position…."[27]

In an artistic vein, the writings of Virginia Woolf, according to historian Laurel Ulrich, "challenged seemingly impermeable boundaries between male [masculine] and female [feminine] identity." Woolf believed that people were, in yin/yang fashion, androgynous, and she illustrated that point by describing a relationship between two cross-dressing people as "a revelation that a woman <u>could be</u> as… free-spoken as a man, and a man [<u>could be</u>] as… subtle as a woman." [emphasis added][28]

Such notions of gender convergence make for good rhetoric and good drama, but they run into the brick wall of gender bias. As historian Judith Wellman put it, "In theory, all women were mothers—or they had been or would be or ought to be." Assertive women like Elizabeth Cady Stanton, the Grimké sisters, Lucretia Mott, and Abby Kelley upset the stable expectations of the proper place of women. Conservative institutions like churches, politics, and journalism did not know how to respond politely to them, so old values became fodder for battles. The old roles had fit into a hierarchy of expectations that made male control easy, but respect for those roles was changing as respect for individual rights ascended.[29]

The point at issue, of course, was power, and the institutional response was vehement. On July 18, 1837 the Congregational General Association of Massachusetts issued a pastoral letter condemning the Grimké sisters for breeching the traditionally passive role of women by entering the political arena of debate and reform. It claimed that such women would find "shame and dishonor in the dust."[30]

The press typically ridiculed women who met in women's rights conventions, characterizing them as "entirely devoid of personal attractions" and resembling "the gatherings of an insane asylum…." Such women were viewed as unsexed "hybrids" or

"Amazons," and men who supported the movement were "she-male" and effeminate.

Some critics even suggested that supportive men wear dresses in order to show the public where they stood on the women's rights issue. Female supporters of the issue were often characterized in masculine terms in order to rationalize their human rights passion. The <u>New York Herald</u> referred to Lucretia Mott as "General" or "Caesar: all bone, gristle, and resolution."

Noting Harriet Tubman's resolution to succeed as an Underground Railroad conductor, John Brown called her "General Tubman."[31]

When the first issue of the radical women's rights journal <u>The Revolution</u> appeared on January 8, 1868 with Elizabeth Cady Stanton as its editor, conservative reaction was bound to follow. Cady Stanton vowed that she would make sure the journal was "charged to the muzzle with literary nitro-glycerine."

The <u>New York Sunday Times</u> editor noted that Cady Stanton would do better tending to "domestic duties," and that Susan B. Anthony should get a "good husband and a pretty baby."[32]

For Cady Stanton, the most irritating source of opposition to the women's rights movement came from women themselves—those who claimed that they already had all the rights they wanted. In a speech at Seneca Falls in 1848 she declared,

> "The most discouraging, the most lamentable aspect our cause wears is the indifference, indeed the contempt, with which women themselves regard our movement. When the subject is introduced among our young ladies… it is met by the scornful curl of the lip and by the expressions of disgust and ridicule…. They… glory in their bondage.
>
> "Resolved, that the women of this country ought to be enlightened in regard to the laws under which they

live, that they may no longer publish their degradation
by declaring themselves satisfied with their present
position, nor their ignorance by asserting that they
have all the rights they want."

Cady Stanton compared such women to the supposedly happy slave, and asked, "Can there be one woman in this nation so
ignorant that she really thinks she is already living in the full possession of all the rights that belong to a citizen of a Republic?"[33]

Other women activists supported Cady Stanton regarding
complacent women, but abolitionists generally remained silent
about it. Susan B. Anthony wrote to a friend in England that
women in the United States were so complacent that it would
require "some terrific shock to startle the women of this nation
into a self-respect [strong enough to] force them to break their
yoke of bondage."

Lucretia Mott said at the Woman's Rights Convention of
1856 in New York City,

> "The assertion of woman that she has all the rights she
> wants, only proves how far the restrictions and disabili-
> ties to which she has been subjected have rendered her
> insensible to the blessings of true liberty."[34]

All of the above radical women would agree that by accepting
the status quo, women legitimated their own subservience. Some
of the more conservative women even subscribed to the late 1840s
fad of Spiritualism as a technique of acquiring feminine power;
they believed that their ability to talk with the dead afforded
them some higher social status, and the ability to advise others.[35]

The one category of women that really galled Cady Stanton
with their conservatism was schoolteachers. A speech she wrote
for Anthony in 1857 dealt with the issue of equal education for

both sexes, and equal pay for female teachers—many of whom objected to it.

> "What an infernal set of fools these school-marms must be. Well, if in order to please men they wish to live on air let them. The sooner the present genera- tion of women dies out the better. We have jackasses enough in the world now without such women propa- gating any more."[36]

As Cady Stanton and Smith learned in their reform work, the interplay of gender and roles is indeed complex. Even though their humane goals were clear, they had difficulty escaping the bounds of traditional biases.

One last example of this complexity involves black males. As the institution of slavery developed in the United States, the need to subjugate black males increased. Until the nineteenth century, gender bias was seldom related to race; but as black males es- pecially began to desire power to escape bondage, gender and race became interlinked. To disempower black males—free and slave—they were depicted as feminine: weak, dependent on oth- ers, and subject to the temptations of passion. They were called "boys" and assigned exaggerated feminine gender characteristics such as economic irresponsibility and eroticism, and not allowed to occupy any positions of importance. True 'manhood' required the suppression of feminine identity, so white males became in- creasingly segregated from other groups.[37]

I conclude this chapter with the thesis from Elizabeth Cady Stanton's "The Solitude of Self."

Diversity among humans does not negate the necessity of equality in human rights. It seems, however, that white males were at least slow, or at most ignorant of understanding this.

The political fact is that people who are discriminated against are aware of the social structures and institutional linkages that create and legitimate it, even though their personal experiences may differ. This puts them in a position to coalesce into a politically powerful force. Because both of the human rights movements covered here—the antislavery and women's rights movements—involve discrimination based in ascription of feminine gender characteristics, their coalescence would be powerful indeed. White males' defense of their assumed vulnerability to disempowerment usurped the huge influence they might have had in aiding the implementation of equal rights for all.

FIVE

Seneca Falls and the Women's Rights Movement

"The history of mankind is a history of repeated injuries and usurpations on the part of man toward woman, having in direct object the establishment of an absolute tyranny over her."
—Elizabeth Cady Stanton and Lucretia Mott
From the Declaration of Sentiments,
Woman's Rights Convention at Seneca Falls, 1848

The attitude expressed in that statement is clear: women were angry, and they were ready to do something about it. Cady Stanton's conversations with Lucretia Mott in London in 1840 had primed the pump. Now, the water was ready to flow.

On June 22, 1847, Daniel Cady had deeded his daughter Elizabeth a house and land in Seneca Falls, New York. She was its sole owner. While she moved from Boston to this new property, Henry stayed behind to finish some antislavery work. He did not arrive at Seneca Falls until February of 1848. Elizabeth had enjoyed her independence, but was becoming bored with domestic chores.

On July 13, 1848 and again on July 16, Elizabeth met in nearby Waterloo with the McClintock family, Jane and Richard

Hunt, Martha Coffin Wright, and Lucretia Mott. They made plans for a Women's Rights Convention to take place on July 19 and 20 in Seneca Falls. They wrote a Declaration of Sentiments modeled after the Declaration of Independence that became the master document to spread the news of what women were up to. Cady Stanton called it "as good a bill of impeachment against our sires and sons as they had against old King George."[1]

The declaration connected the women's rights movement with an unfinished American Revolution, just as antislavery documents had done before it. It recognized a problem based in bias and manifested in authority and power. The "cult of domesticity" that it challenged rested in the presumed natural differences between men and women that justified different roles and expectations, and had resulted in customs and laws that reinforced the subordinate role of women.

The call for the convention was published in the Seneca County Courier on July 11, and in Frederick Douglass' North Star on July 14. Douglass, an avowed abolitionist, saw the connections between the two movements and answered Elizabeth McClintock's invitation to attend,

> "To be sure I will do myself the pleasure of accepting your kind invitation to attend the proposed woman's convention at Seneca Falls."[2]

Cady Stanton called the convention "the most momentous reform that had yet been launched on the world—the first organized protest against the injustice which had brooded for ages over the character and destiny of one-half the [human] race." She commented that it was held to protest

> "... laws which make [woman] the mere dependent on [man's] bounty [and to have] such unjust laws...
> forever erased from our statute books, deeming them a

standing shame and disgrace to a professedly republican people in the nineteenth century."

This comment sounds much like what Gerrit Smith said about slavery in a speech at the New York State Capitol on March 11, 1850:

> "What a wonder, what a shame, what a crime, that, in the midst of the light and progress of the middle of the nineteenth century, such an abomination and outrage as slavery, should be acknowledged to be a legal institution."[3]

Both cousins realized the impact that the advances of science and reason were having on individual minds and on the social structure. The revolutionary shift from isolated villages to networked mega-communities was changing lifestyles from conformity to existing institutions to radical attempts to change those institutions to meet new needs. Cady Stanton and Smith were both determined to use their personal resources to foster that change through reform.

The philosophical essence of the reform initiated formally at Seneca Falls revolved around the principles of the reasoning capacity of women, their just place in a political democracy, and their natural rights based in one's individual being. Women were becoming increasingly angry about the constrictive roles assigned to them by men in power. The verbs that they used in the resolutions passed at the 1848 convention reflect that anger: "compelled," "never permitted," "withheld," "deprived," "taken," "framed," "usurped," "monopolized."

The influence intended from the Seneca Falls convention was aimed at moral change—a change of attitude—in the general population. Both Cady Stanton and Smith started their reform work using this "moral suasion" approach. Their basic belief was optimistic: when people were persuaded of their sins regarding the oppression of others, they would opt for change.

Cady Stanton stated it clearly:

> "I would give more for the agitation of any question on sound principles, thus enlightening and convincing the public mind, than for all the laws that could be written or passed in a century."

When their efforts at persuasion produced little progress, both turned to political efforts to change the rules. Importantly, both understood that changes in the rules that govern personal behavior regarding discrimination would not change the score of the game. That goal of eliminating sexism and racism would devolve upon future generations.[4]

The convention ignited, as Wellman aptly states, "a revolution of women against patriarchical institutions: the law, the family, religion, work, education, and... politics." Public reaction was mixed, but mostly negative.

Most of these institutions were dominated by men who saw no benefit to themselves in the women's rights movement, and attempted, said Cady Stanton, to "make our movement appear... ridiculous." Only those journals edited by abolitionists approved of the women's effort. The North Star, edited by Frederick Douglass, and The Liberator, edited by William Lloyd Garrison, printed favorable responses. Cady Stanton and Elizabeth McClintock wrote to the editors of the Seneca County Courier three days after the convention:

> "If your columns are open to the women of Seneca county, we throw down the glove to any one who will meet us, in fair argument, on the great question of Woman's Rights. Depend upon it, this soon will be

the question of the day. All other reforms, however important they may be, cannot so deeply affect the interests of humanity, as this one. Let it therefore be fairly and candidly met. Ridicule will not have any effect on those who seriously feel themselves aggrieved; argument is far better."

Other responses reflected the bias of the male editors. The Philadelphia Public Ledger and Daily Transcript noted that "A woman is nobody. A wife is everything." The Rochester Advertiser called the convention "a most insane and ludicrous farce." In Albany, Mechanic's Advocate claimed that "if men were to share equally in domestic duties [it would] prove a monstrous injury to all mankind."

The Oneida Whig lamented,

"Was there ever such a dreadful revolt?... This bolt is the most shocking and unnatural incident ever recorded in the history of womanity. If our ladies will insist on voting and legislating, where, gentlemen, will be our dinners…?"

Even though Horace Greeley, editor of the New York Tribune, was sympathetic to antislavery issues, he could not empathize with women, and only reluctantly conceded their suffrage goals saying, "However unwise and mistaken the demand, it is but the assertion of a natural right, and such must be conceded."[5]

Following this women's rights convention in Seneca Falls in 1848, the movement did not immediately take off. Women's energies were largely absorbed by child-rearing, housekeeping duties, and commitments already in progress in the antislavery movement. Although annual national women's rights conventions started in 1850, Cady Stanton did not attend most of them.

She did some writing for newspapers during that time, but only after 1860 did her active participation and oration inspire the movement.[6]

The fact that we must talk and write about 'women's rights' or 'African-American rights' or 'gay rights' reveals the fundamental problem Americans have with the idea of 'natural rights'. If we really believed that all people are created equal, such specific 'rights' concepts would not be necessary.

Bias, however, has led us to create a very unequal world in which liberal-minded people strive to redress the grievances of those who are oppressed, and in which the oppressed themselves loudly and sometimes violently demand change.

Gerrit Smith was liberal-minded, but not oppressed. Elizabeth Cady Stanton was both. She initiated the women's rights movement as a response to the clash between her growing sense of self-empowerment and society's demands for subservience. The essence of her argument was that women should acquire governance over their physical and social being—"self-sovereignty," as she put it. Her goal, as she stated in the "History of Woman Suffrage," was "to rouse women to some sense of their natural rights as human beings, [and] to their civil and political rights as citizens of a republic."[7]

That task, however, would be difficult to achieve, and she knew it. "The Pioneers in the work for the redemption of women," she wrote, "found an unbroken field, not fallow from lying idle, but arid and barren, filled with the unyielding rocks of prejudice and choked with the thorns of conservatism." The reason for this was that this "field" was the territory of males, and as women violated it, the males rallied to defend their turf.[8]

Cady Stanton wrote about the way that men treated women,
"... it is enough to rouse one's blood to the white heat of rebellion against every 'white male' on the Continent.

> When I think of all the wrongs that have been heaped
> upon womankind, I am ashamed that I am not forever
> in a condition of chronic wrath,… my lips overflowing
> with curses, and my hand raised against every man and
> brother."

She was so disgusted with arrogant, egotistical men who talked a lot that she preferred "a man who can hear but cannot speak, if [there is] one constructed on that plan."[9]

Her focus for the movement was on the tyranny of social customs that disempowered women. She was dismayed that

> "courage and self-reliance [are] educated <u>out</u> of the
> [young] girl, her path portrayed with dangers and
> difficulties that never exist…. The best protector any
> woman can have, one that will serve her at all times
> and in all places, is <u>courage</u>."

In a culture with a representative government, that courage should gird one for the struggle with male legislators. In a country with no revered figureheads such as king or queen, crown or nobility, law is venerated as the symbol of rightness and justice. Women, then, should guard against its legitimation of *in*justice.[10]

In an address to the New York State legislature, Cady Stanton invoked what she and her cousin Gerrit called the "self-application principle" to test the validity of laws:

> "We ask no better laws than those you have made for
> yourselves. We need no other protection than that
> which your present laws secure to you…. We ask for all
> that you have asked for yourselves…."

Cady Stanton called the attention of institutional leaders to the point that,

> "whenever any class is subject to fraud or injustice,
> it shows that the spirit of tyranny is at work, and no
> one can tell where or how or when the infliction will
> spread...."[11]

And to arrest the spread of that "tyranny," she knew that all women would need to be sensitized to their poor quality of treatment.

> "Women will never claim their civil rights, until they
> know their social wrongs."

That sensitization would be a difficult process because of the power inherent in the male-supported biases that created and legitimated female inferiority. To encourage people to perceive those biases throughout the culture she asked,

> "Is the bondage of the priest-ridden [woman] less
> galling than that of the slave because we do not see the
> chains, the indelible scars, the festering wounds, the
> deep degradation...?"[12]

As a mentor and ally in this formidable public education process, Cady Stanton hoped that she could rely on her "dear cousin" Gerrit Smith. After all, he had introduced her to Iroquois matriarchal culture and worked for years for the emancipation of slaves. Her respect for him was clear when on September 18, 1845 she named her third son Gerrit Smith Stanton. Henry wrote to Gerrit, "If the prospects are that he will not make a great man, we shall change his name."[13]

Smith's spoken and written positions on women's rights looked good. One of his main charities was integrated educational institutions, which he viewed as a means of equalizing differences among all people. He called the refusal to allow women to speak in public a "violation of benevolence and common sense." At the National Woman's Rights Convention in Syracuse in 1852, he stated,

> "These women… do not ask favors; they demand
> rights, the right to do whatever they have the capacity
> to accomplish,… and to have a voice in the laws and
> rulers under which they live."

This certainly sounded positive, but he added, "I make no claim that woman is fit to be a member of Congress or President; all I ask for her is what I ask for the negro, a fair field." So his "fair field" was tainted with prejudice that he would not apply to white males.[14]

He did recognize the philosophical similarity between the sexes:

> "I would have no characteristic delicacy of woman, and
> no characteristic coarseness of man. On the contrary,
> believing man and woman to have the same nature,
> and to be therefore under obligation to have the same
> character, I would subject them to a common standard
> of morals and manners." Except for the biological
> differences related to childbirth, "man is woman, and
> woman is man."[15]

Sensing something rotten in Smith's statement, Cady Stanton snapped back that his "twaddle about the essential oneness of man and woman… makes woman a slave." Her reasoning was that this assumption equated the two sexes, thereby putting women in the position of being as prejudiced and arrogant as the men.[16]

Smith did support the women's movement in ways that made him feel comfortable. He sent donations of money to Cady Stanton; he supported liberal newspapers that favored women's rights;

he contributed money to women's rights organizations and con-ventions; he signed the calls for their conventions; and he wrote letters of support to be read at such meetings in his absense.[17]

Although he seldom attended women's rights meetings, he was often invited. The leaders of women's conventions wanted to have his name associated with their effort. Lucy Stone wrote,

> "We want to make [our convention] tell gloriously for the cause of human freedom—and to this end we want the best helpers on that occasion. We want Gerrit Smith. His very name and approving presence will do us good." And Susan B. Anthony pleaded with him, "I do so want your name associated with this meeting...."[18]

Smith thought his support of women's rights to be sincere, but Cady Stanton had questions about it. He had written to her that he thought she was one "whose views are most in harmony with my own...." But Cady Stanton saw his support as being only financial and rhetorical. His philosophical position was clear, but not supported by his actions.[19]

One way to judge the rhetorical quality of a man's statement about women was to observe how he treated the women in his family. In Smith's case, he was at times condescending toward his wife Ann, and his daughter, Elizabeth. He would not allow Ann to have any money of her own until late in her life, and he would not approve of divorce. When Elizabeth wanted a new home and an elegant wedding, Gerrit balked at supporting both. Yet his greatest exposure of honesty regarding the women's rights movement appeared in an 1855 letter to Cady Stanton in which he answered her challenge to his support.

In fairness to Smith, it must be noted that his skepticism regarding the potential for short-term success of the women's rights movement was not a personal disapproval of its goals, but a cultural analysis of its efficacy. That is, he believed that people should pursue equal rights for women, but "the present age" was just not the best time for it.

Given his optimism for the success of reform efforts in other movements such as temperance, peace, tobacco use, and the abolition of slavery, it seems odd that he would throw a blanket of pessimism over women's hopes. But we must remember that his thought was dominated by practical considerations, and he did not believe that the powerful pieces of the puzzle could come together at this point in time for assuring the success of the women's rights movement.

Early in that 1855 letter, Smith stated his personal philosophy: "The object of the 'Woman's Rights Movement' is nothing less than to recover the rights of woman…. I say nothing against this object. It is as proper, as it is great…."

And because of his concern that people were not ready for it: "You would [want to] know why I have so little faith in this movement…. [The fact as I see it is that] tradition and chivalry and a misinterpreted and superstitious christianity [are] in the way of this cause."

What he saw was that solid traditions of male dominance, supported by long-standing custom and the power of religion, could not allow such liberal ideas as women's rights to gain legitimacy. And—importantly—many of those people supporting such power and traditions were women. As Cady Stanton had pointed out, many women were satisfied that they had all the rights they wanted.

Given these headwinds, and looking back in retrospect, Smith's analysis of the probable lack of success of the movement was prophetic. Yet it did not go over well—especially with the eager, angry, and impetuous Cady Stanton.

Regarding the leadership of the women's rights movement, Smith claimed

> "that it is not in the proper hands; and... the proper hands are not yet to be found.... My sorrow is, that they, who are intent upon it, are not capable of adjusting themselves to it—not high-souled enough to consent to those changes and sacrifices in themselves, in their positions and relations, essential to the attainment of this vital object."

And at this time in 1855, one can cite the rejection of the bloomer dress reform effort by both the larger culture and by women themselves as evidence that Smith was right.

To fortify his position, Smith continued in this letter: "

> But if there is not enough compass of mind and nobility of soul—not enough of strong common sense and bravery and self-sacrifice, in our age, to furnish the necessary bands of reformers against Intemperance and... Slavery, certain it is, that it must be left to another age to furnish the reformers who are competent to carry the cause of women to victory. For, it must be remembered, that the success of this cause will involve more comprehensive, and radical, and difficult changes than will the success of all those other reforms put together."

He saw other reforms, such as the temperance and antislavery movements, as involving a smaller portion of the population and fewer institutional areas than did the women's rights movement. Also, public bias against change in women's roles was more intense than that against others. There were, he noted, antislavery people in both the North and the South, but too many people of both sexes throughout the country opposed changes in the roles of women.[20]

Cady Stanton responded to Smith's letter with disgust. She knew of all the powerful forces arrayed against achieving equal rights for women, but she was not as pessimistic as her cousin regarding success. Even though she knew that many women were reluctant to become actively involved in the movement, she held hopes that her persuasive work could stimulate widespread help— especially among women. As she saw it,

> "they alone whose souls are fired through personal experience and suffering can set forth the height and depth, the source and center of the degradation of women; they alone can feel a steadfast faith in their own native energy and power to accomplish a final triumph over all adverse surroundings…."

Men, she felt, could not empathize enough with women to understand the intensity of their emotions regarding oppression. Most of them would agree with Smith that women were too weak to face the forces opposing them. Her response to Gerrit reflected her disgust:

> "You say you have but little faith in this reform, because the changes we propose are so great, so radical, so comprehensive; whilst they who have commenced the work are so puny, so feeble, and underdeveloped."[21]

She essentially shook her finger at what she saw as his conservative and prejudiced face for having asserted that "As soon as [woman] shall consent to place herself under the instructions of reason and common sense," she will achieve the changes desired.

And, of course, he would be glad to dictate to her the proper reason and "common" sense.[22]

Smith's latent bias against women showed up in other places, too. In an 1849 philanthropic land give-away deal, he had originally required that the financially poor recipients "must... be taken from the sexes in equal numbers." But when it appeared that his supply of available land might be short, he concluded "that it is not best for the females to receive land...." One must ask, why not the males?[23]

The early and radical female abolitionist Angelina Grimké once refused an invitation to appear at an antislavery meeting with Gerrit Smith and Lewis Tappan because, in her view, they did not support women's rights positions. Cady Stanton viewed as hypocrites those reformers who held republican principles yet continued to betray women by maintaining dominance over them. To this point, she railed,

> "Can it be that here, where we acknowledge no
> royal blood, no apostolic descent, that you, who have
> declared that all men were created equal—that govern-
> ments derive their just powers from the consent of the
> governed, would willingly build up... an aristocracy
> that would raise the sons above the mothers that bore
> them?"[24]

Clearly, Elizabeth Cady Stanton had a long-standing disgust with males' tyrannical use of power. To fully understand her view of the rights of women and their social potential, one must comprehend her connection early in life with Native American culture in central New York State.

The young Elizabeth Cady's first extensive contact with Native American culture probably occurred during her long summer visits with her cousin, Gerrit, in Peterboro in the 1830s. Gerrit's father, Peter, had close contact with the Native American Oneida tribe during his business dealings with them in the fur trade in the late 1700s and early 1800s. After Peter founded Peterboro and made his residence there in 1806, the friendly Oneidas were frequently present at his home.

Both Gerrit and Elizabeth Cady had contact with them and learned about their social structure. About seventy percent of native North American cultures were characterized by a form of government called either a gynocracy (female rule), or a matriarchy (mother rule). The Oneidas were one such group.

Some researchers of the women's rights movement have noted that this model of gynocracy in Native American life was missed or ignored by local residents due to the prejudice of northern European settlers toward them. Sally Wagner claims that this "suppressed history" retarded the development of the movement. And as Paula Allen put it,

> "The price the feminist community must pay because it is not aware of the recent presence of gynarchial societies on their continent is unnecessary confusion, division, and much lost time."[25]

Oneida culture saw a natural balance among gender roles. Men were the hunters and women were the producers. Women were responsible for both the biological production of the clan, and the agricultural production of food. Because of their responsibility for long-term reproduction and short-term sustenance, women acquired respectability and power.[26]

Being sensitive to natural rhythms, the Oneidas understood that ecological processes produced balance or stability amid a diversity of types and species. "Variations," they believed, "make for a more beautiful planet," especially when all varieties and differences are treated with respect. Because women's responsibilities were respected, they felt a "wonderful sense of freedom and safety," and were not threatened with abuse. The Christian beliefs of most European immigrants devalued women by assigning them non-productive and non-governmental roles, thereby robbing them of respect. Within the Native American gynocracies, the high status of women made it a privilege for others to mimic them, so male cross-dressers "who crossed standard gender lines were considered important members of the community and often held in very high esteem." They were called "berdaches" in the Native American language, and were respected as people who were capable of integrating genders.[27]

Probably the most important aspect of the gynocratic culture was the characteristic of women as political rulers. The Oneidas believed that because nature had endowed women with the ability to create life, they should be in a position of power to protect that function. As custodians of life, women encouraged deep respect for "Mother Earth," while the main concern of men was the protection of the women. Because women were most sensitive to the character of other people, they chose the clan's titular leaders from the male population. The clan mother nominated candidates whom she believed did not want or seek political power. The chief was then selected by the women. The candidate for chief had to be one who was

> "free from such motives as greed, a lust for power, envy, and malice, [and was able to] see beyond his time and be willing to enact only laws and policies that protect the sovereign rights of the people for seven generations to come."

No campaigning for the position was allowed.[28]

Laws passed under the chief's authority should be designed to protect the rights of clan members for the next two hundred years, or seven generations, in order to ensure continuity of the culture. If the quality of leadership of the chief was in question, women retained the power to recall him.[29]

Respect for women was also evident in the marriage relationship. The Oneidas believed that the worst of crimes were those perpetrated against women. A husband who had beaten his wife faced punishment by the entire community. He was required to run through a two-line gauntlet of women armed with clubs. The resulting scars served as a lifetime stigma. A male rapist was branded on his face with a recognizable mark and banned from his community.[30]

With these types of cultural rules in place in Native American cultures, it is not surprising that the first married woman's property law was passed in response to the model set by local Chikasaw people in Mississippi in 1839. Also, because women worked the land for agricultural production, they were considered to be in control of it, so all land sales and treaties had to be negotiated with them.[31]

Early women's rights advocate Matilda Joslyn Gage summed up the position of women in Native American culture:

> "Its women exercised controlling power in peace and war…. No sale of lands was valid without consent of the women, while the family relations among the Iroquois demonstrated woman's superiority in power…. In the home, the wife was absolute…. If the Iroquois husband and wife separated, the wife took with her all the property she had brought [and] the children also accompanied the mother, whose right to them was recognized as supreme." If a marriage was sustained, "all real property [was] held by the bride. The husband [was] considered to be living in her home, on her land."[32]

With this type of culture to observe at Peterboro, the young Elizabeth Cady learned of the huge differences between European American and Native American beliefs and practices regarding women:

Native American	European American
Female spiritual being	Male god
Women choose leaders	Women have no vote
Women hold property	Women own no property

The challenging question that Cady asked was, "Why not us!?" And although it took a few years to develop, her answer was to launch the women's rights movement.

By the 1840s, Elizabeth Cady Stanton was ready to light the fuse of change that had been extinguished after the American Revolution. In 1776, Abigail Adams wrote to her husband John as he worked at forming a new nation,

> "be more generous and favorable to [women] than your ancestors…. Do not put… unlimited power into the hands of husbands…. We are determined to foment a rebellion, and will not hold ourselves bound by any laws in which we have no voice or representation."

But the revolutionary theme of equality was not extended to African Americans or women, and was left to later generations to pursue. Women, Cady Stanton claimed, had become brainwashed to accept their own subservience. When in public meetings with women, she commented,

> "… it was impossible for conversation to rise above the wash-rag level! It was enough to make [one] 'solemn' to see such a wreck of glorious womanhood."

When only men were allowed to speak and vote in some meetings, Cady Stanton was disappointed "to look into the faces of women and see that by far the larger proportion were perfectly satisfied with the position assigned to them."[33]

This resigned attitude and servile position of women was common to many cultures throughout the world. Even though she was eager to pursue the women's rights movement, Cady Stanton viewed this attitude as a severe impediment to its success. As she put it,

> "Whether our feet are compressed in iron shoes, our faces hidden with veils and masks, whether yoked with cows to draw the plow through its furrows, or classed with idiots, lunatics, and criminals in the laws and constitutions of the state, the principle is the same, for the humiliations of spirit are as real as the visible badges of servitude. A difference in government, religion, laws, and social customs makes but little change in the relative status of woman to the self-constituted governing classes, so long as subordination in all nations is the rule of her being."

She claimed that "Thus far women have been mere echoes of men…. The true woman is as yet a dream of the future. A just government, a humane religion, a pure social life await her coming."[34]

The tactics supported by Cady Stanton to pursue these dreams were based in the process of social networking. She knew from having watched the abolitionists that the power to produce change would accrue through the coalescence of many groups, political parties, and individuals with similar interests. Like cousin Gerrit, she did not want to drop out and revolt, but would rather reform the existing institutional structure.

In the early days she held "conversationals" at her home where men and women came together to eat, dance, exercise, and talk about new issues and directions for women. This was an inexpensive way for women to become involved, as they had little money of their own to fund the movement. Cady Stanton's home in these early days was sometimes referred to as "the center of the rebellion." Frequent visitors were activists such as Lucretia Mott and Abbey Kelley.[35]

The real power base for the movement began to develop in the 1850s with the advent of conventions and national organizations. The first convention to be held following the July 1848 Seneca Falls meeting was in Rochester, New York only two weeks later on August 2. Organized by Amy Post, it continued the discussions of women's rights issues.

Surprisingly, Lucretia Mott and Cady Stanton refused to sit on the platform with convention president Abigail Bush because it would break the tradition of male leadership of public meetings. Cady Stanton later apologized for that action, claiming that she was having difficulty watching women in that role. She quickly lost that anxiety.[36]

The first national women's rights convention was held at Worcester, Massachusetts on October 23 and 24, 1850. It was organized mainly by abolitionists who recognized the theme of oppression and the demand for equal treatment. Frederick Douglass attended, and from the Gerrit Smith family, Ann Smith, Gerrit, Elizabeth Smith Miller, and Charles Dudley Miller signed the call for the convention. Another major convention occurred in Syracuse, September 8-10, 1852. It was one of the few women's rights meetings attended by Gerrit Smith. Susan B. Anthony referred to it as a "brilliant galaxy of men and women [discussing women's rights from] every conceivable stand point."[37]

As usual, press reactions to these early meetings were often negative. The proslavery <u>Syracuse Daily Star</u> announced the impending convention:

> "The women are coming! Mighty will be the force of 'jaw-logic' and 'broom-stick ethics' preached by the females of both sexes."

And then, about the meeting, the <u>Daily Star</u> reported: The "Tomfoolery Convention" resulted in a

> "... silly rant of 'brawling women' and Aunt Nancy men,… most of them… Abolitionists of the most frantic and contemplable kind,… preachers of such damnable doctrines and accursed heresies, as would make demons of the pit shudder to hear."

The next day, the paper apologized for publicizing

> "... the mass of corruption, heresies, ridiculous nonsense, and reeking vulgarities which these bad women have vomited forth…. The proceedings of these three days' pow-wow… awaken burning scorn for the participants in them."

The <u>New York Herald</u> on September 12 called the convention "The farce at Syracuse," attended by

> "mannish women, like hens that crow… having the same vein as the fanatical Abolitionists…. Of the male sex who attend these Conventions… the majority are hen-pecked husbands, and all of them ought to wear petticoats."[38]

Another major technique of networking was the establishment of national organizations. After the Emancipation Proclamation had attracted more public interest in ending slavery in early 1863,

Cady Stanton and Anthony issued "An Appeal to the Women of the Republic" to gather in New York City in May to assess the issues of abolition and women's rights. Following two days of meetings, the National Women's Loyal League was established with Cady Stanton as president and Anthony as secretary. Its main interest was the emancipation of slaves, as women honored their verbal commitment to abolitionists to postpone the pursuit of feminist goals until after the war.

The League disbanded in August of 1864 having collected over 400,000 signatures on petitions in support of the thirteenth amendment to abolish slavery. Even though women's rights was not its main focus, the League helped women learn how to organize themselves and network with the public, and aided in their development of self-respect and confidence.[39]

After the Civil War and the refusal of male political leaders to include women in the fifteenth amendment that enfranchised black males, organizations supporting woman suffrage appeared. The National Woman Suffrage Association was established in New York City on May 15, 1869 with Cady Stanton as president and Anthony as chair of the executive committee. Its objective included not just suffrage, but equal rights for women in all areas of life. A competitive organization, the American Woman Suffrage Association was founded in Cleveland on November 24, 1869 with Henry Ward Beecher as president and Lucy Stone as chair of the executive committee. Its focus was on suffrage only. Whereas the "National" advocated federal action to achieve its goals, the "American" focused on state action to achieve the vote for women.[40]

When these two major organizations had difficulty cooperating, and when factions and discord occurred within them, Cady Stanton became disgusted with them and gave up on organizations as an effective way to pursue goals. During the 1870s, she became active on the lecture circuit and spent several months each year traveling and speaking. These organizational difficulties within the women's rights movement were reminiscent of similar troubles that plagued the abolition movement in the 1840s.[41]

By the late 1880s, the futility of maintaining two antagonistic national organizations was addressed by rival leaders Lucy Stone and Susan B. Anthony with the result being a merger of the "National" and "American" associations in February of 1890. The new National American Woman Suffrage Association elected Cady Stanton as president, Anthony as vice president, and Stone as chair of the executive committee.[42]

Addressing legislators directly was another technique that Cady Stanton used in her decades-long effort to secure equal rights for women. She made addresses before the New York State Legislature on February 14, 1854 and February 18, 1860 that challenged the ability of men to make laws that recognized the "violence done to… woman."

> "The slaveholder cannot make just laws for the slave; neither can man make and execute just laws for woman, because in each case, the one in power fails to apply the immutable principles of right to any grade but his own…."

To the legislators, she reviled "The Tyrant Custom" telling them that "the daughters of the revolutionary heroes of '76, demand at your hands the redress of our grievances…."[43]

The slow progress toward equal rights for women aggravated Cady Stanton as she grew older. She saw it as a manifestation of the seemingly immutable bias of men against women. At the July 4, 1876 Centennial celebration in Philadelphia, she was denied permission to read the Woman's Declaration of Sentiments, but Anthony walked onto the speakers' platform and read it anyway.

The managers of the event constructed a separate Woman's Pavilion for the women's exhibition. Cady Stanton remarked,

> "The Woman's Pavilion upon the centennial grounds was an afterthought, as theologians claim woman herself to have been.... To many thoughtful people it seemed... unreasonable for women to complain of injustice in this free land, amidst such universal rejoicing."

The men present assigned the women's protests to "unfortunate individual idiosyncrasies" instead of the oppressive social conditions.[44]

By the 1880s, the only major advance in women's rights that Cady Stanton could cite was the 1848 New York State law that granted property rights to women. The passage of this law occurred after twelve years of legislative debate, and, as she realized, was passed in large part because the male aristocracy in control of the state legislature was selfishly concerned about their daughters' wealth being lost to unrelated males upon marriage. The property issue also highlighted an interesting aspect of male power and control.

Until the early 1800s, male power, identity, and a stable psychological sense of self emanated from the possession of hard cash (gold) and physical property. After 1830, as the source of wealth changed from cash to speculation (paper "money"), one's sense of financial and psychological stability vanished. Power slipped away as money changed from gold and silver treasure to speculative capital. Manhood was fiscally imperiled and masculinity lost. As men lost their grip on the sword of gold, they felt feminized and humiliated. This drove them toward new techniques for maintaining power and control such as concern that their female family members not lose property to alien males, and making sure that the power of the vote belonged to males only.

The problem was that for centuries men had had a fetish-like relationship with "treasure" (which is what Henry Stanton actually called Elizabeth Cady!). After 1830, their sense of self became variable with shifts in the stability of the economic market. Fiscally secure manhood dissolved in a shower of "panics," so men resorted to new tactics to secure their power. As Cady Stanton saw it,

> "Husbands in extensive business operations could see the advantage of allowing the wife the right to hold separate property… that might not be seized for his debts."

So allowing one's wife or daughter to hold property removed some of the insecurity of possession that had developed in the new speculative economy. As one incurred debt, it produced feelings of inferiority, humiliation, and submission. Ownership was undermined as the basis of individuality, identity, and manhood. No longer having the ability to control what they owned, men turned to attempts to maintain control over their political status because they were already in control there.[45]

Other signs of slow progress in the movement included the fourteenth Amendment, and the actions of major political parties. The fourteenth Amendment to the United States Constitution was designed to assure "equal protection of the laws [to] citizens of the United States." Cady Stanton pointed out that these "citizens" were defined three times in the amendment as "males," a fact that questioned the citizenship of women. Then, when the Republican Party held its presidential nominating convention in 1872, it had split into two factions. The newer faction called the "liberal" Republicans met in Cincinnati and nominated the anti-women's rights candidate Horace Greeley. The "regular" Republicans met in Philadelphia and nominated U.S. Grant for a second term. His re-election platform included a plank which noted that equal rights for women should receive "respectful consideration." Cady Stanton disgustedly called it a "splinter."[46]

Such actions by male dominated institutions assured Cady Stanton that the battle for "self-sovereignty" and equal social and political rights would drag on. She began to see slavery not as a metaphor for the female life, but as the very condition of it. And, as with slavery, it was not the *right* of a woman to rebel, but her *responsibility* to do so. Women's responsibility to implement freedom was not to man, but to God. As her cousin Gerrit Smith had said, "To no human charter am I indebted for my rights."[47]

The women's rights movement was also deterred by having their friends and mentors, the abolitionists, either die of old age or pull away as they pursued equal rights for black males after the Civil War. As Cady Stanton said to Anthony in 1869, "You and I know the conflict of the last twenty years; the ridicule, persecution, denunciation, detraction, the... bitterness of our cup for the past two [years], when even friends have crucified us." The abolitionists were also aggrieved when Cady Stanton and Anthony published The Revolution in 1868 with the financial backing of George Train, a noted Democrat and racist.[48]

The lack of support even extended to some women's organizations. The Women's Christian Temperance Union, founded in 1873, did not support the tactics or ideas of the more radical Cady Stanton and Anthony, who knew as they worked for equality that the movement was becoming more conservative as a result of opposition. Cady Stanton had said of men, "how like feudal barons you freemen hold your women." She claimed that "Society as organized today under the man power is one grand rape of womanhood," and that "Married women are… servants without wages."[49]

In spite of some gains made by women after the war—some jobs and colleges opening up to women, suffrage in a few local elections, full suffrage in the territories of Wyoming and Utah—Cady Stanton realized that the bias of men against women was so entrenched that it would not change quickly. In the face of such conservatism, she speculated in the 1880s that without men in power giving "serious consideration" to equal rights for women, conciliation would wane and violence would become a live option. Her progression of thought is very similar to that of her cousin Gerrit relative to the abolition of slavery.[50]

In her later years as the suffrage theme grew more important, Cady Stanton graduated beyond just that to the bigger picture of the oppression of women by men in economic, political, and religious institutions. Her wholistic social reform theme, however, lost out in the late 1800s to Anthony's emphasis on suffrage, thus limiting the long-term influence of the movement. Once the vote was achieved in 1920, the women's rights movement went dormant for decades, not understanding itself as part of a human rights movement. As Cady Stanton understood, "suffragism" was not "feminism." The result of achieving the vote was that Susan B. Anthony received historical credit for victory while Elizabeth Cady Stanton was ignored. This secured the subservient status of women for decades to come. It amounted to a cheap victory for men; a power move that did not emancipate women or change the score of the social game.[51]

But our purpose here involves more than coverage of the woman's rights movement alone, so let us examine how it was related to the antislavery movement.

SIX

Links Between the Antislavery Movement and the Women's Rights Movement

"Standing as we do upon the [summit] of human freedom, we can not be deterred from an expression of our [support] of any movement, however humble, to improve and elevate the character of any members of the human family…."
—Frederick Douglass, <u>The North Star</u>, July 28, 1848

So said escaped slave and abolitionist Frederick Douglass one week after having attended the first women's rights convention in Seneca Falls, New York. He could see clearly the similarity in the emotional reaction to oppression felt by slaves and by women. Boston abolitionist William Lloyd Garrison had said just two years earlier, "I am bound to use my powers for the welfare of the whole human brotherhood."[1]

Generally, abolitionists believed that the moral improvement of society was their responsibility. Their support for the oppressed who were disempowered by the patriarchal institutions of the day was grounded in self-sacrifice, so they contradicted many nineteenth century values that defined masculinity. Instead of endorsing self-interest and individualism, they advocated self-sacrifice, civic virtue, independence of thought, equality, and justice. The cause of social oppression, they thought, was not to be found in immutable individual physical or genetic characteristics, but in a changeable cultural environment that reinforced distinctions that led to inferiority. Believing that they could do something about such distinctions, they embarked on a reform effort that would eventually include not just slaves, but women as well.

In 1829, early abolitionist Benjamin Lundy hired Elizabeth Margaret Chandler as editor of the Ladies Repository section of his journal, the Genius of Universal Emancipation. She seized the opportunity to advocate that women become involved in antislavery activities, such as boycotting the products of slave labor, sponsoring public lectures, and petitioning Congress. Abolitionists, however, were generally cool to female participation in the movement because they feared that it would deflect public attention away from the main issue of the abolition of slavery, and because their own positions of superiority might be challenged. This concern over the participation of women in their work was reflected many decades later: when the aging abolitionists wrote their memoirs in the 1870s and 1880s, women were seldom mentioned.[2]

There were some abolitionists who rejected male dominance. They were generally recognized as "Garrisonians"—the followers of Boston journalist William Lloyd Garrison. With the focus on the rights of others as their ethos for human action, they had less difficulty seeing connections between oppressed groups of people than did those who were more mired in the cultural stereotypes of the time.

When women first became involved in antislavery activity, they did so on men's terms. But fund raising and petition drives became boring, and revealed to them their clash with entrenched male power. Although the antislavery movement drew men and women together as they focused on a common enemy, it also enlightened women to the source of their own oppression, and stimulated them to launch a human rights movement of their own. Elizabeth Cady Stanton stated this connection well:

> "In the early Anti-Slavery conventions, the broad principles of human rights were so exhaustively discussed, justice, liberty, and equality so clearly taught, that the women who crowded to listen, readily learned the lesson of freedom for themselves, and early began to take part in the debates and business affairs of all associations."

She called the antislavery movement a training ground for the women's rights movement where women learned how to establish their own organizations, write constitutions, develop management skills, communicate with the public, raise and manage funds, and network with legislatures, politicians, and journalists.[3]

Female antislavery societies were established as early as 1833, and the first Women's Anti-Slavery Convention occurred in New York City on May 9-12, 1837. Chaired by Lucretia Mott, it drew seventy-one delegates from seven states, one of whom was Ann C. Smith of Peterboro. The meeting provided women the opportunity to prepare resolutions, design a petition drive, and raise funds. Although these were weak accomplishments, this was the first interracial, public, and politically oriented meeting of American women.

Press reaction was typical. The New York Commercial Advertiser called them "misguided ladies… who put aside their frying pans to debate weighty matters of state." The church-based Congregational General Association of Massachusetts expressed "regret [for] the mistaken conduct of those who encourage females to bear an obtrusive and ostentatious part in measures of reform."[4]

In spite of public reaction, many women and some men became "crossover representatives" of both movements. British abolitionist George Thompson said of the early woman reformers in 1835, some "females of America are nobly devoting themselves to this work of mercy, regardless of the malignity of their heartless... persecutors."

Interestingly, African-Americans of both sexes who were active in the antislavery movement were more receptive to the idea of women's rights than were the white male leaders, with African-American women in particular being ultra-sensitive to the issue because of their "double-jeopardy" position of being both black and female. Women at the first National Woman's Rights Convention at Worcester, Massachusetts in October of 1850 resolved as follows:

> "That the cause we are met to advocate,—the claim
> for woman of all her natural and civil rights,—bids us
> remember the million and a half of slave women at the
> South, the most grossly wronged and foully outraged
> of all women; and in every effort for an improvement
> in our civilization, we will bear in our heart of hearts
> the memory of the trampled womanhood of the
> plantation, and omit no effort to raise it to a share in
> the rights we claim for ourselves."

We should ask: Is that all that black women should get— just a "share" in the rights that white women are seeking? There appears to be some latent racism in that statement. Today, we recognize that black women epitomize the issues of racism and sexism: recent biographies have resurrected the reputations of both Sojourner Truth and Harriet Tubman.[5]

In examining some "crossover" persons, we find early Garrisonian abolitionist Abby Kelley clearly stating the connection between the movements:

> "We have good cause to be grateful to the slave for the benefit we have received to ourselves in working for him. In striving to strike his irons off, we found most surely that we were manacled ourselves, not by <u>one</u> chain only, but by many. In every struggle we have made for him, we find we have been also struggling for ourselves."

In the 1850s, Kelley traveled to Ohio to protest "black laws" that had been passed there in an effort to prevent fugitive slaves from passing through the state. In her public speeches, she also encouraged women to develop self-respect and enter into the human rights battle.[6]

Angelina and Sarah Grimké also became well-recognized "crossover" figures. Originally from a slave-holding South Carolina family, these sisters moved to Philadelphia and broke social barriers to become public speakers in the antislavery movement. Angelina was the more effective orator. Between May and November of 1837, she spoke at eighty-seven locations to over 40,000 people. Just through the act of speaking in public, she became an advocate of women's rights. She wrote to Catherine Beecher in 1837,

> "When I look at human beings as moral beings, all distinction in sex sinks to insignificance and nothingness; for I believe it regulates rights and responsibilities no more than the color of the skin or the eyes."[7]

Male reaction to the Grimké sisters' public speaking was mixed. Pro-slavery writers characterized them as "moral monsters" or "would-be men." Perhaps they saw some correlation there. In 1836 when Gerrit Smith was president of the New York State Anti-Slavery Society, he questioned the appropriateness of their public speaking proposal, fearing that it might become a "Fanny Wright affair." Frances (Fanny) Wright was a British abolitionist and women's rights activist who was stigmatized and ignored as a reformer because of her advocacy of birth control. Smith did finally change his opinion and provide financial support for the Angelina Grimké speaking tour. The Grimké sisters were chosen as the only two women of "The Seventy," a group of abolitionists trained by the American Anti-Slavery Society to be itinerant speakers.[8]

Lucretia Mott was also noted for her view of antislavery and women's rights as being two aspects of the same human rights movement. Her formative years took place among Quakers on Nantucket Island. Because men were often absent at sea, women conducted both family and business affairs amid a social climate that posed no implications of inferiority. A young Lucretia observed this equality of the sexes among her elders and her peers— similar to what Elizabeth Cady experienced with the Oneidas— and developed serious skepticism concerning the value of male dominance.

Her notion that legitimate authority emanated from "truth" led her to question sources of authority that claimed to know the truth, such as domineering males either as slaveholders, husbands, or priests.

The early abolitionists knew Mott as a committed antislavery worker, so her later identification with women's rights lent credibility to that movement. In an interesting interaction with Gerrit Smith, she chastised him for his expenditure of large sums of money for the purchase of freedom for individual slaves. Smith did it because he liked to see quick, visible results of his philanthropy. Mott saw it as "misdirected benevolence," and an "indirect support of slavery" because it legitimated the existence of the institution. But in the long view, Mott was optimistic regarding the prospects for progress in human rights issues. "The spirit of Freedom," she said, "is arousing the world."[9]

When Lydia Maria Child published her "History of Woman" in 1832, it was just a first step in her human-rights work. This three-volume history of the condition of women established her reputation as a fearless human rights advocate. Her link between the two movements discussed here became evident in 1833 with her publication of "An Appeal In Favor of that Class of Americans Called Africans." She knew that its anti-racist theme would bring her "ridicule and censure," but said, "Should it be the means of advancing, even one single hour, the inevitable progress of truth and justice," then it would be worth the price.

The Philadelphia African-American businessman James Forten recognized her "Appeal" as a great book because of its daring anti-racist theme. She condemned prejudice against people of color, and wrote eloquently about the long and proud history of African people. Child wrote,

> "To the last hour of my life my voice and my pen shall be given to… [human rights] work…. For this cause I wish to live—for this cause I am willing to die."

As early as 1838 in a letter to Angelina Grimké, Child realized that persuasive efforts to alter public morals would not work, and that violence would become necessary to address human rights concerns.[10]

Frederick Douglass found that the support of both antislavery and women's rights ideas coexisted well. Women's complaints of male dominance resonated with his memories of oppressive treatment as a slave. Douglass gleaned positive impressions of strong women from his early relationships with his mother and grandmother. According to his biographer,

> "For the rest of his life, Douglass looked to women as
> confidants, companions, and sources of strength. They
> rather than men could be comprehended and counted
> on to be able."[11]

Douglass also attributed his early enthusiasm for women's rights to conversations with Elizabeth Cady Stanton. "Observing woman's agency, devotion, and efficiency," he said, "in pleading the cause of the slave, gratitude for this high service early moved me to favorable attention to the subject of what is called 'woman's rights.'" He felt proud that as a young man he had been able to overcome selfish concerns about liberty for himself and "for my people," and extend empathy to women. As he put it, "when I stood up for the rights of women, self was out of the question and I found a little nobility in the act."

His respect for women showed clearly when he wrote in his autobiography,

> "When the true history of the Anti-Slavery cause shall
> be written, women will occupy a large space in its
> pages; for the cause of the slave has been peculiarly
> woman's cause. Her heart and conscience have supplied
> in large degree its motive and mainspring. Her skill,
> industry, patience and perseverance have been wonder-
> fully manifest in every trial hour...."

It was not that Douglass did not appreciate the human rights work of men like Gerrit Smith, Garrison, Brown and others, but that he especially noted the effort of women to be unswerving as they faced intense issues of discrimination themselves.[12]

This partial list of "crossover people" illustrates some early connections between the two human-rights movements. It could include many others such as Boston's Maria Weston Chapman, who contributed her expertise to antislavery journals, fairs and conventions; and Harriet Beecher Stowe, whose "Uncle Tom's Cabin" stirred nationwide interest in both slaves' and women's issues. And there is, of course, one other person who deserves mention as part of the connective tissue between the two movements: Elizabeth Cady Stanton.[13]

Elizabeth's first moving contact with human rights issues occurred in Peterboro. There she met runaway slaves, Native Americans, and abolitionists who whetted her appetite for concern about oppression. She referred to herself as having "been trained in the school of anti-slavery." Such training primed her for meeting Lucretia Mott, whom she described as "a broad, liberal thinker on politics, religion, and all questions of reform [who] opened to me a new world of thought." They met in London at the 1840 World Anti-Slavery Convention, an event that was the catalyst for the women's rights movement in the United States. From that point on, Cady Stanton pursued what she might have called a "melded movement," emphasizing at various times the goals of one movement or the other.[14]

On their return from London in late December of 1840, Elizabeth and Henry spent part of the winter living with the Smiths in Peterboro. Elizabeth stated the hope that "Cousin Nancy" (Gerrit's wife Ann) would help her learn more about antislavery work so that she could be supportive of her new husband's concerns. Ann was seldom active in reform activity, but she did play the important role of consistent domestic support of her husband's work. Abolitionist Parker Pillsbury once wrote that he hoped historians of the antislavery movement "will not forget these heroines of the fireside."[15]

As Cady Stanton matured in reform work, she saw that "the prejudice against sex was more deeply rooted and more unreasonably maintained than that against color." Prejudice against sex, she claimed, was easy to overlook or to perceive as natural because it was so pervasive. "A married woman," she said, "has no more... rights than a slave on a Southern plantation." She used this analogy to make women aware of their own subordination and oppression, and to arouse their indignation. It was a recruiting tool. She would point out that although a slave could escape, a woman could not.[16]

While living in Chelsea, near Boston, in the mid 1840s, she interacted with a lot of women's rights and antislavery activists, and noted the need for uniting the two movements. Her networking efforts were aimed not at "the African slave alone, but to the slaves of custom, creed and sex as well...." She saw the big picture of reform as a "question of religion, philanthropy, political economy, commerce, education, and social life on which depends the very existence of this so called republic."[17]

Cady Stanton's philosophical allegiance to factional attitudes regarding questions of human rights appears as something of a puzzle, but it is a solvable one. In one way she was "Garrisonian," because that school of abolitionism encouraged and accepted the participation of women. But she disagreed with Garrison's ideas regarding the use of politics and the vote. That is, she saw the activity of women in efforts at moral suasion as necessary in achieving the public attitude to establish *liberty* for all, and, at the same time, she saw political participation by all citizens as necessary in achieving *justice* for all.

So—if we were to achieve our Constitutional ideals of Liberty and Justice for all, she would need to be eclectic and support both factions. She became, therefore, a fan of Garrison's attitude toward women, and of Smith's attitude toward politics.

Because of the influence of her father as a lawyer, her husband as a politician and Gerrit Smith as a reformer, Cady Stanton understood that law was the major force in legitimating and maintaining the tyranny of white men, and that political equality would allow the oppressed slaves or women to struggle collectively against oppressors instead of individually against one man. This practical orientation to her thought allied her more closely with the Smith school of abolition than with that of Garrison. "I am in favor," she said, "of political action, the organization of a third party, as the most efficient way of calling forth + directing action." "A party formed and candidates nominated [would] give a reality to antislavery principles." To conclude, Cady Stanton's philosophical position regarding reform was eclectic. Mentally and rhetorically she supported Garrison, but she always saw practical value in supporting Smith's ideas of political and legal action, which Garrison opposed.[18]

Her approval of Garrison's thoughts about women is not surprising. They were together at the 1840 London conference when its British managers refused to seat the eight female delegates from the United States. Britain had abolished slavery in 1833, and the conference was called to discuss that success and the techniques for achieving it elsewhere. Because the significance of social class was higher in Britain than in the United States, and because women were considered to be a lower class than men, the issue of seating the women seemed to British men "a most trifling matter." "It was," Cady Stanton said, "really pitiful to hear narrow-minded bigots, pretending to be teachers and leaders of men… cruelly remanding… womankind, to absolute subjection…." She questioned

> "the sincerity of abolitionists who, while eloquently defending the natural rights of slaves, denied freedom of speech to one-half of the people of their own race.

Such is the consistency of an assemblage of philanthropists!"

Garrison, Henry Stanton, and Wendell Phillips refused their
seats there as delegates, and spoke out against the British action.
Elizabeth remarked,

"Those who had learned the first lessons of human
rights from the lips of... Gerrit Smith would not accept
any such position."[19]

With no formal organization representing the women's rights
movement in the 1840s, it depended for support and promotion
on the antislavery movement. Garrisonian organizations such
as the New England Anti-Slavery Society and the American
Anti-Slavery Society did offer women a vehicle for expression
of their discontent with the "domestic cult," but some members
thought women's rights to be "an irrelevant topic," and worried
that it would detract from the power of their abolition message.
Although Garrison remained loyal to his pledge to allow female
participation, most male members of these groups were patronizing toward women, viewing them as member-servants who
could help to compensate for male arrogance and impetuosity.
Even Garrison segregated their writing that he published in The
Liberator to a "Ladies Section."[20]

The efforts of women to organize a power base for antislavery
work illustrates their subordinate status in the nineteenth century. The fact that they had to establish sex-segregated female organizations was symptomatic of their rejection by those in power.
Once established, their goals were often more moral than practical because most people, including many females, did not expect
that women would, or could, become political. For example, the
Pennsylvania Female Anti-Slavery Society was established a few

days after the American Anti-Slavery Society began operating in December of 1833. Prestigious female leaders such as Lucretia Mott, Abby Kelley, and the Grimké sisters were active in it, yet when they met in convention in 1838 at Pennsylvania Hall in Philadelphia, the public's reaction was to burn the building in which the women spoke.[21]

When the American Anti-Slavery Society met for its annual meeting in New York City in May of 1839, there was an internal debate over whether women should be counted in the roll of those present. Gerrit Smith chaired the meeting and supported the women, who won the right to be counted by a vote of 184 to 141. The vote clearly showed the strength of the force opposing female participation.[22]

Another example of organizational disconnect between the sexes occurred during the Civil War. As an effort to emphasize emancipation as the goal of war, Henry Stanton and Gerrit Smith organized the Loyal National League in May of 1863. Their target was the Democrats who claimed that reunification was the goal. As a supportive response, Elizabeth Cady Stanton and Susan B. Anthony organized the Women's National Loyal League.[23]

These split organizational tendencies illuminate a disturbing aspect of the connections between antislavery and women's rights activities: Men felt threatened by women. These males who were enlightened, educated, liberal, benevolent philanthropists built a human rights movement based in morals that rejected selfish motives and actions—unless they were their own.

In the 1830s and 1840s, educated women generally felt a moral responsibility to aid the oppressed. They supported the antislavery movement and wanted to be active in it. But white males excluded women from participating in their organizations because it threatened to undermine their superiority in the patriarchal social structure. Power-hungry males needed to rationalize their subordination of women, so they found supportive work for the women to do. They shunted them into tasks that offered the illusion of having political importance in the movement without bothering the men or threatening their presumed importance. Women became "helpers" in the work toward black emancipation without diluting the power of the entrenched males.[24]

Women could feel empowered, the men hoped, by holding bazaars and fairs to raise money to support men's groups. The annual antislavery fair sponsored by the Philadelphia Female Anti-Slavery Society occurred during the Christmas season, and sold "free" produce and antislavery items that had been made and donated by the women. The fair raised an average of $1500 per year (over $112,000 in today's currency) starting in 1835. The money was donated to male antislavery societies, vigilance committees, and journal editors.[25]

Women also led the effort to boycott the products of slave labor. The idea was that if there were no market for such products, the institution of slavery would wither. However, support for such products, and for the institution of slavery itself, was too solid in the North for a boycott to have much effect. William Lloyd Garrison called it "a waste of time," and the American Anti-Slavery Society refused to endorse it. The Gerrit Smith family tried to honor the boycott idea in the 1830s, but had difficulty locating replacement products. Cady Stanton once asked her friend Elizabeth Smith about her baby brother Greene's clothes: "Did you find his antislavery wardrobe abundantly supplied?" Elizabeth Smith did feel proud about using "free produce" in their home.[26]

Women were also encouraged to gather signatures on antislavery petitions. They disliked their work, but did it anyway as a substitute for the absence of real political power in the movement. They spent huge effort over many thousands of hours collecting hundreds of thousands of signatures on petitions that male members of Congress intentionally ignored by passing a "gag rule" that automatically tabled them upon receipt.

By these techniques, women worked hard and stayed out of the way of the male managers of the movement. And, ironically, accepting these roles amounted to a condoning of male domination. Their labors did little more than to, as Cady Stanton said, "second man's endeavors, and exalt his sex above her own."[27]

There have been some isolated attempts to see women's work in the antislavery movement as productive. Friedman's contemporary analysis suggests that women acquired training in organizational work and experience in leadership management. The argument is that this alleviated feelings of alienation and gave them a personal sense of importance, empowerment, and assertiveness, and created visibility for women.

Right! And where were the power and influence they desired?[28]

In one interesting twist on this theme, it was the encouragement of female reformers like Lydia Maria Child and Lidian Emerson in the Concord, Massachusetts area that eventually persuaded the reluctant transcendentalist Ralph Waldo Emerson to join the antislavery movement. But generally, the power of women in organizational work was squelched during the antebellum era. One of the major symptoms of this was the split—the schism, some called it—in the ranks of antislavery people that occurred in 1840.[29]

The "woman question" drove a wedge into the log of abolitionism. William Lloyd Garrison and his "Boston clique" of followers favored the participation of women in public life. His dominant technique of pursuing the abolition of slavery was "moral suasion"—the attempt to convince pro-slavery people that slavery was a sin. Tactics involved public speaking and journalism. Because he believed the Constitution to be a pro-slavery document, he disapproved of political activity and voting as a means toward change. And even if politics could succeed in abolishing slavery, it would only be a change in the laws instead of a change in people's minds. Racism would still exist, making emancipation meaningless.

The Garrisonian focus on the necessity of moral change before political change made the employment of women in the movement a reasonable idea. After all, women were stereotypically more moral than men, and would be naturally committed to such a process. This is ironic: Garrison's opinions regarding women are often interpreted as being liberal, but he was conservatively banking on them to fulfill their domestic stereotype of being the family's (or the movement's) moral leaders.

In opposition to this Garrisonian approach stood those abolitionists who had grown tired of wasting time and energy through moral suasion. They had become aware of the intensity of the cultural bias that discriminated against blacks and supported slavery—especially in the North—and they were opting for political action through a third-party effort. Many clerical leaders also opposed Garrison's ideas about women because they feared the radical image of women opting for public attention or political power would dilute the message about slavery.[30]

The two camps included the moral suasionists led by Garrison and the political activists led by Gerrit Smith and Lewis Tappan, an abolitionist businessman from New York City. When these opposing sides met in May of 1840 at the annual meeting of the American Anti-Slavery Society, the stage was set for a clash of opposing ideas. Garrison had stacked the body of voting delegates with his followers from Massachusetts, so the result was predetermined.

As the meeting progressed, Abby Kelley was nominated for a seat on the business committee, and approved by a vote of 557 to

451. Kelley immediately became a symbol of female participation in public life, and about 300 of those opposed to this idea left the meeting to form the American + Foreign Anti-Slavery Society. Led by Smith and Lewis Tappan, this new organization was in favor of political action to achieve abolition, and because the specter of women as public figures sparked reactionary responses and inflamed male members, they were discouraged from active roles.

Cady Stanton reacted predictably:

> "Whilst with one hand, they strove to loose the chains that clanked on the rice plantations in Georgia, with the other, they tried to force woman back into the niche [of restricted duties, and crush] her first efforts to rise above the clouds of prejudice…."[31]

The fact that the American Anti-Slavery Society was now firmly under the control of the Garrisonian Boston clique did not bother the recalcitrant Smith group. They were already building a new base of power in the Liberty Party, and saw no need to network with the Garrisonians, who encouraged people not to vote.

The "woman question" was prevalent in antislavery circles all the way to the Civil War. Even within some female groups, there was dissension about the proper role of women. The Boston Female Anti-Slavery Society, although racially integrated, debated the issue. The press belittled women who spoke in public as "petticoat politicians," and recommended that they return to their kitchens. Cady Stanton noted,

> "We may date the Woman's Rights movement in this country to the division in the Anti-Slavery ranks in 1840."[32]

This insight lends major significance to the schism in the antislavery movement. Garrisonianism had provided major impetus for the antebellum emergence of the women's rights movement, a fact that moved the concept of reform from tinkering with drinking habits on an individual level to reformulating the normative foundation of western culture. It is at this turning point that our two major characters emerge onto the national stage as prominent radical thinkers.

Elizabeth Cady Stanton was injected into the antislavery movement by Henry B. Stanton upon their marriage in 1840, and she quickly became embroiled in the human rights issues of concern to both blacks and women. She wrote to Gerrit Smith from London, "The thought that three millions of our fellow beings and countrymen groan in bondage... is enough to sadden any heart." And her empathy for women in "bondage" was also soon evident.[33]

Gerrit Smith, meanwhile, emerged from the schism as the leader of a national movement toward a third political party. He became more visible to the public, and he congealed his thinking into a pragmatism that would eventually make him one of the most powerful and effective abolitionists in the country.

The over-arching, big-picture perspectives of both Cady Stanton and Smith led them to support various strategies in their reform work. This fact may lead to confusion in the minds of some readers, but one must keep in mind the depth of empathy that characterized both of them. For instance, it may seem to be a mystery why Gerrit Smith would so intensely favor the emancipation of slaves, yet ally himself with the American + Foreign Anti-Slavery Society that opposed the participation of women in public life. His practical analysis of the social forces pressing upon issues at the moment was so keen that he could place his support at the critical point for assuring the greatest possible degree of success. It was not that he did not empathize with and support women's rights, but that—at that moment—

he felt that his resources could be most effectively used in a parallel cause.

As an example of his adaptive, eclectic and inclusive thought, in 1843 Smith invited Abby Kelley, a dedicated Garrisonian, to conduct an antislavery speaking tour at his expense in central New York State. He believed her to be an excellent orator and a superb representative of the human rights cause, and he was trying to mend the rift between the Boston and New York factions within the antislavery movement. In non-empathic fashion, she wrote back to him,

> "You do not realize what you ask at my hands. It is nothing less than to identify myself with the Liberty Party…. Is it possible that you can ask me to cooperate with those who have been so traitorous to the slave's cause, who would trample me in the dust because I am a woman?"[34]

In like fashion to Smith, Cady Stanton could empathize with Garrison's acceptance of women, and still work toward emancipation through the Liberty Party. Both were able to adapt to prevailing circumstances by melding seemingly contradictory ideas. One result was that both of them remained aloof from national antislavery organizations. As Smith wrote to the Weld-Grimké family,

> "Like yourself, I can go neither with the Old or New Antislavery Organization at the present. I am sick, heart sick, of the quarrels of abolitionists between themselves."[35]

The empathy expressed by both male and female abolitionists did not characterize the general population of that era. The prejudices of those in charge of most major social institutions—white males—abounded against anyone who was not like them.

The fable called "history" is told by those who are power-ful—the winners, the white males—for their benefit. They create acceptable myths and a usable past that will serve their preference to stay in power, such as: how the West was 'won'; Jesus Christ was white; the United States is a land of liberty. By this myth-building process, whole groups of people have been omitted from historical writings, or discriminated against to the extent that current generations are led to believe that they were unimportant, undeserving of respect, or simply outsiders to be ignored.

The fifth-century BC Greek playwright Euripides wrote in the play, "Hippolytos," "women are a huge natural calamity, against which men must take strenuous measures." He specu-lated that men needed a way to make babies on their own. Plato declared in "Timaeus" that women existed to punish men, and Aristotle considered women to be useful only for reproduction.

The Bible considered women to be an afterthought of cre-ation, with Eve vulnerable to serpents and pain and legitimately dominated by her husband. Even early social contract theorists in the 1700s omitted women: John Locke claimed that female infe-riority was a natural plan involving the dependency and weakness of women. Jean Jacques Rousseau regarded women as existing to please men, having no desire for their own independence.

Such conceptions of women both reflected and legitimated culturally designed inequalities that made it possible for other groups to remain in positions of dominance. Self-definition of superiority is a self-fulfilling prophecy built on characteristics or traits selected by the dominant group. The recognition of a dif-ference is interpreted as evidence of inferiority, with the assump-tion that subordination is legitimate. This phenomenon has had varied applications over past centuries.

Before 2000 BC, female sex was considered to be a perma-nently inferior ascribed status. Slaves were typically women of captured cultures because of their reproductive ability, while men were killed as a threat to the captor's dominance. In these ancient times, skin color was recognized as a result of climate, and generally not considered to be important in determining one's status. Racial inferiority was deterred by the reluctance of men to degrade some of their own type.

In the 1700s, naturalists began to classify plants and animals into taxonomic groups, thus encouraging the classification of people into human varieties. Probably because the early scientists were white males, they speculated that this must be the dominant group. People who were inferior needed guidance by those who were 'naturally' capable of governing. These, of course, were white males; thus the violence inherent in slavery and marriage.

The problem of assigning slave status to skin color was solved by feminizing black males. The problem emerged as follows: If women historically were considered to be naturally inferior and subject to slavery, how could black males logically be enslaved? The answer involved transferring feminine gender characteristics to black males. The feminine gender traits previously discussed— weakness, submissiveness, emotionality—were attributed to black men, thereby making them classifiable with women. The dualistic (we/they) pattern of western European thought, then, enabled those in power to use a clear gender-based distinction to categorize people into superior or inferior groups, making it culturally legitimate to subjugate women and black men to a white male master. White males needed easily visible biological characteristics on which to judge and evaluate to maintain their superior position. They successfully bundled women and black men into one group based on gender stereotype, thereby providing themselves with a rationalization of dominance.

What had happened was that the habit of Europeans to think in opposites—dual patterns like hot or cold, black or white, good or bad, superior or inferior—transferred easily to alien cultural types. The emphasis on ascribed, biologically based characteristics when combined with gender to determine inferiority was effective at obscuring selfish motives of white male superiority.

With these distinctions in place, 'race' became a primary symbol of inferiority by the middle of the eighteenth century. The possibility of stripping power from large cultural groups was accomplished as white males assigned feminine gender 'inadequacies' to anyone who was different, then required them to submit to their power through institutions such as the plantation, the state, the family, and the church.[36]

Today, with the advent in the twentieth century of "civil rights" laws in the United States that offer some legal protection against prejudicial discrimination toward African Americans, women are rightly pointing out that sex and gender discrimination is, as was the case historically, more prevalent than that against race.

The power of long-standing cultural norms to maintain patterns of discrimination cannot be denied. Even the most radical abolitionists could not overcome that pressure, as they found traditional gender roles difficult to reject.[37] During her sea voyage to London in 1840, Elizabeth Cady Stanton talked at length with Liberty Party presidential nominee James G. Birney about the "woman question" regarding their participation in public life. She learned he was upset with "the women who had fanned the flames of dissension, and had completely demoralized the anti-slavery ranks." Throughout the 1840s and 1850s, pro-slavery advocates picked up on the persistence of this cultural pattern and its long history, claiming that if it was legitimate to treat women as inferior people, then similar treatment of slaves was justified.[38]

A disturbing result of the power of this cultural tradition was that it was supported by law. "Status of the mother" laws linked slavery with sex as a degrading feature, and marriage laws degraded women who were linked with blacks. A 1664 Maryland law condemned to slavery for her husband's lifetime any white woman who married a black slave, and a 1723 Virginia law provided that "any woman who bore mixed-race children would become legally black."[39]

When white schoolteacher Delia Webster aided the escape of a slave from Kentucky in 1844, she was arrested and brought to trial. Governor William Owsley refused to pardon her, saying, "We insist upon her punishment not only on account of the offense she has committed, but because of her sex, which she has desecrated." His discriminatory application of law is clear.[40]

Both Cady Stanton and Smith worried over the effect of law upholding discrimination against women and blacks. In an address to the American Anti-Slavery Society, Cady Stanton noted that slavery had "corrupted our churches, our politics, our press,… it has gagged our statesmen, and stricken our Northern Senators dumb in their seats; yes, beneath the flag of freedom, Liberty has couched in fear."

And Smith, in a letter to Cady Stanton, wondered about some abolitionists and legislators: "What can they do toward overthrowing slavery, whose endeavors to that end are… neutralized by their admission that slavery can be embodied in law—real, obligatory inviolable law [as in the Constitution]."[41]

To highlight the tendency of a judicial system to uphold discriminatory laws, women's rights activists Elizabeth Smith Miller, Susan B. Anthony, and Elizabeth Cady Stanton all became involved with a Pennsylvania court decision to execute a woman for having committed infanticide. An all-male jury had sentenced Hester Vaughn to death. She had been abandoned by her husband to an unheated house in the winter. When Miller, Anthony, and Smith presented the governor with a petition defending Vaughn, he pardoned her due to lack of evidence.[42]

Probably the most galling institutional support for discriminatory treatment of women and blacks, especially as far as Cady Stanton was concerned, was the church. She felt that women were treated

> "just as slaves were.... The clergy were the most bitter
> opponents to the public action of women.... Among the
> clergy we find our most violent enemies—those most
> opposed to any change in woman's position.... Woman
> in her present ignorance is... like the poor slave 'Uncle
> Tom,' her religion, instead of making her noble and
> free,... has made her bondage but more certain and
> lasting, her degradation more helpless and complete."[43]

Christian churches and their leaders generally emphasized individual conduct and belief as a means of acquiring personal salvation and everlasting life. They did not view the church as an institution that should be pursuing the moral reform of society, because such an effort would produce internal dissension and the loss of support from church members. This position was the antithesis to reform. For example, in 1845, the Presbyterian General Assembly refused to issue a resolution regarding slavery because it preferred to avoid "all divisive and schismatic measures tending to destroy the unity and disturb the peace of the church."

Regarding the hesitancy of most Christian churches to support human rights issues, Abby Kelley designed a pledge that she offered at her public speeches obligating people to support "immediate and unconditional emancipation." Those who signed it recognized oppression of others to be "a heinous sin and crime...." She was pleased that the pledge "throws corrupt politicians and [church] sectarians into most delightful spasms."[44]

To sum up the connections between the antislavery and women's rights movements, we must take a brief look at their relationship to the Civil War. Both the abolitionists and the women's rights activists knew by the mid 1850s that civil war was inevitable. In 1856, Cady Stanton wrote to Elizabeth Smith Miller that she was convinced that "violence, blood, and civil war" was imminent. "Our fair republic," she wrote, "must be the victim of the monster, slavery, unless we speedily rise in our might and boldly shout freedom." Gerrit Smith had seen war coming since the late 1840s.[45]

The serious question for women was which movement should they support; where should they place their efforts—with the slave, or with women?

Matilda Joslyn Gage said of the war,

> "Unless liberty is attained—the broadest, the deepest,
> the highest liberty for all—not for one set alone, one
> clique alone, but for man and woman, black and white,
> Irish, Germans, Americans and Negroes, there can be
> no permanent peace."

It was a dilemma. Although women knew that their liberty was worth fighting for, they realized that the Civil War had been caused by slavery, and that now they had to choose. Among women there was an undercurrent of optimism about supporting the war with its goal of emancipating slaves. They felt that if they worked hard to support the abolitionists, the favor would be returned after the war. The abolitionists had by 1861 gained power enough to destabilize the institution of slavery, and women's rights leaders like Cady Stanton looked forward to having that force placed behind their goals.

Abolitionist Theodore Dwight Weld had advised the Grimké sisters to back off on demands for women's rights until the slave was free. Lucretia Mott had stated that her first loyalty was to the rights of the slave.[46]

In accordance with this drift of thought, Cady Stanton agreed that she, too, should support the primacy of the emancipation of slaves. In fact, she leaned so far in that direction that she sounded as if she was deferring to the men:

> "So long as one slave breathes in this Republic, we drag the chain with him. God has so linked the race… that all must rise or fall together…. Let the men who wield the nation's power be wise, brave, and magnanimous, and its women will be prompt to meet the duties of the hour with devotion and heroism."[47]

In the early stages of the war, Cady Stanton tried to help the cause by speaking in public against slavery. But her enthusiasm waned when she saw how President Lincoln was conducting the war. She believed, as did Smith, that his emphasis on reunion of the nation ignored the more important issues of human rights. Smith called Lincoln's war policy "twattle and trash."

Cady Stanton wrote to Elizabeth Smith Miller,

> "I do hope the rebels will sack Washington, take Lincoln, [Secretary of State] Seward, and [Union General] McClellan and keep them safe in some Southern fort until we man the ship of state with those who know whither they are steering and for what purpose."[48]

In general, human rights activists in both movements were disappointed with Lincoln's reluctance to emancipate slaves. And even when he did so on January 1, 1863, it only applied to some of the slaves, and occurred as a necessary military tactic instead of as a moral choice. It appeared to active reformers that "the men who wield the nation's power," as Cady Stanton had put it, cared more about their own positions than they did about human rights. The advice of the women and the abolitionists was ignored. For the abolitionists, this pill was not too bitter to swallow; they knew that their goal of the abolition of slavery was at hand. For the women, however, it reinforced their determination to press harder, and made them wonder how long it would take before those in power would listen. Lydia Maria Child had stated the point well:

> "When a man advises me… not to act according to the dictates of my own judgment, I am constrained to reply: 'Thou canst not touch the freedom of my soul.'"[49]

When slavery was completely abolished by the ratification of the Thirteenth Amendment on December 18, 1865, Cady Stanton was less thrilled than she was worried. She noted that

> "the black man is [now], in a political point of view, far above the educated women of the country…. Are we sure that he, once entrenched in all his inalienable rights, may not be an added power to hold us at bay?"[50]

If she needed any further proof that women were not being heard, it came from the reunion of abolitionists nine years after the Civil War. When they met in Chicago in June 1874, the women used the opportunity to rally some of the old abolitionists' reform enthusiasm to the cause of women's rights. Two of the speakers, women's rights activist Rebecca W. Mott and abolition journalist Jane G. Swisshelm, aggravated men in attendance by suggesting that they should pay more attention to helping women achieve their goals. The aging abolitionists "almost unanimously declared that the women's rights scheme was not properly before them." The message: the men could *still* not hear the women.[51]

Knowing this, women were no less determined to pursue what they felt they deserved as they embarked on their continuing fight for equality.

Elizabeth Cady Stanton with her sons Henry (left) and Daniel. c. 1848.
Photo courtesy of Coline Jenkins.

This photograph of Stanton was taken shortly after she organized the National Woman Suffrage Association in 1869.
Photo courtesy of Coline Jenkins.

Gerrit Smith and his wife, Anne, in the early 1870s.

From the author's collection.

Gerrit Smith's daughter, Elizabeth Smith Miller, with her young daughter, Anne, around 1860. Elizabeth became an ardent supporter of Elizabeth Cady Stanton's work.

From the author's collection.

(Left to right) Elizabeth Smith Miller. Elizabeth Cady Stanton, and Anthony. *Photo courtesy of Coline Jenkins.*

Henry Brewster Stanton at age 80 in 1885. He was 35 years old when he married Elizabeth Cady in 1840 over the objections of her father, Daniel, and cousin, Gerrit Smith, both of whom thought the courtship had been too brief. She was 24.

Photo courtesy of the New York Historical Society

Born more than 18 years apart, Smith and Stanton shared a passion for social justice. Smith was photographed in 1874, the year he died at the age of 77. Stanton's picture was taken a few years before she died at the age of 86 in 1902.

Photos courtesy of the author and the Peterboro Historical Society.

PART II

Reform Issues Within the

Antislavery Movement

and the

Women's Rights Movement

SEVEN

Dress Reform

"The physiological results of woman's fashionable attire [in-cluded] the crippling effect of tight waists and long skirts, the heavy weight on the hips, and high heels, all combined to throw the spine out of plumb and lay the foundation for all manner of nervous diseases."
—Elizabeth Cady Stanton, "Eighty Years and More, 1898.

The reform issues covered in Part II extend through a time period that includes the decades before and after the Civil War. Whereas Smith and Cady Stanton were intensely involved in activities related to the war during the 1860s, their commitment to reforms other than the abolition of slavery only paused.

As a part of the women's rights movement, the interesting issue of dress reform erupted briefly in the 1850s. The significance of dress reform rests in the point that it was a minor issue with major implications. The different positions regarding dress reform for women revealed men's attitudes toward both women and themselves, exposing a latent prejudice against women.

Even liberal men exposed deep naïveté in believing that a change in dress style would result in a change in attitudes toward and treatment of women—that changing the rules could change the score.

In all cultures, identity is a function of 'passing'. That is, one adopts a cluster of particular ethnic mannerisms, dress styles, and traditions in order to reinforce one's identity as masculine, feminine, rich, Irish, French, or whatever. Stage actors learn well how to do this in order to project a convincing role.

People understand how to interact with those around them in daily life by quickly assessing the meaning of 'props', the visible symbols of role. When these props do not match the static characteristics of a long-accepted role, observers are thrown off balance and are not sure how to react. For instance, if women dress like men or if men dress like women, traditional response patterns to the persons themselves seem inappropriate. The resulting uncertainty and confusion can lead to ridicule, derision, or anger.

The observer's reaction reveals his or her biases. If that observer is liberal-minded enough to *see* those biases and to question whether they are logical and legitimate, the result is, at the very least, tolerance; at the best, it is acceptance. If the observer does not consider the matter and simply reacts on an emotional level, then anger, ridicule, and rejection are likely to occur. This is what some women faced when, in 1851, they opted for "bloomers."

At the time, bloomers were such a radical change in the style of dress for women that they created an almost vicious public reaction. The outfit consisted of a below-the-knee length dress with a pair of pants underneath that fully covered the legs. Some men considered bloomers to have a masculinizing influence on women, and they saw them as a form of cross-dressing. Gerrit Smith's daughter Elizabeth is credited with designing bloomers in 1850, but when Amelia Bloomer wrote about them in her publication, The Lily, the new outfit took on her name.

Gerrit was instrumental in getting his daughter to debut the new style. Concerning the older, socially accepted full-skirt dress style, he had written to Cady Stanton,

> "I hazard nothing in saying that the relation between the dress and degradation of an American woman is as vital as between the cramped foot and degradation of a Chinese woman. This dress does... unfit the wearer for the vast majority of human pursuits...."

Although Smith did see the bulky dress as a symbol of woman's degradation instead of its cause, he seemed to lose sight of the cultural causes behind it as he criticized women's inflexibility. He likened women wearing long dresses while they demanded equal rights to a nation that cut off one hand of every newborn child while declaring "all the wealth,... rights,... respect, and... independence" that it deserved. Women, Smith believed, voluntarily handicapped themselves. The long dress, he wrote,

> "...leaves them less than half their personal power of self-subsistence and usefulness, [and amounts to] voluntary imprisonment and... self-degradation. They are content in their helplessness and poverty and destitution of rights.... The great change which is indispensable, in order to get and enjoy what they demand, is a change in themselves."

Smith thought that if women could only agree to resist the cultural norms and dress differently, men's opinions and expectations of them would change:

> "Only let woman attire her person fitly for the whole battle of life,... and all the nonsensical fancies about her inferiority to him [will disappear]."[1]

This practical type of thought was typical of Gerrit Smith. He wanted to see visible results of his work quickly, and he believed that he could achieve them by targeting the influence of his resources properly. In this case, his resource was not money but advice, and the target was the static minds of women. He might as well have blown on the embers of a fire; when liberal-minded, reform-oriented women heard him, they exploded.

Cady Stanton snapped back, "We have no reason to hope that [pants] would do more for us than they have done for man himself. The Negro slave [wears pants], yet in spite of his dress… he is still a slave." She was disgusted with his simplistic analysis of the issue of female inferiority. "To him," she said derisively, "the whole revolution in woman's position turned on her dress."[2]

Other women also responded to Smith's position regarding dress reform. Journalist Frances D. Gage groused,

> "He has made the whole battleground of the Women's Rights Movement her dress…. This argument, had it come from one of less influence than Gerrit Smith, would have been simply ridiculous. But coming from him, the… oracle of a large proportion of our reformers, it comes worthy of an answer…. [He claims that] garments of men or women govern and control their aspirations [and] that 'women are helpless'."

Obviously peeved at Smith's naïveté, Gage asked, "What reduces both the woman and the slave to this condition? [It is] the law which gives the husband and the master entire control of the person…."[3]

Sarah Grimké reacted to Smith by telling him that she liked the practicality of the bloomers for work and "when the walking is wet." Then she complained:

"I entirely dissent, my dear friend, from your affirma-
tion that the 'Woman's Rights Movement is not in
the right hands.' Surely you must admit that many of
the noblest, most independent, most morally exalted,
most highly cultivated, most comprehensive minds are
engaged in this reform…."[4]

Smith certainly caused turmoil among women's rights advocates with his observations of what he felt were their inadequacies.
The dress that was the object of concern was the floor-length,
hooped dress that restricted freedom of movement. Cady Stanton
remarked that "woman can never be developed in her present
drapery, she is a slave to her rags."

In an eloquent statement on its deficiencies, she noted,

"The most casual observer could see how many pleasures
young girls were continually sacrificing to this dress: In
walking, running, rowing, skating, dancing, going up
and down stairs, climbing trees or fences, the airy fabrics
and flowing skirts were a continual impediment and
vexation. We can not estimate how large a share of the
ill-health and temper among women is the result of the
crippling, cribbing influence of her costume."

She even believed that the dress could "lay the foundation
for all manner of nervous diseases," and that "it seemed as if… a
rational costume for women [should] be an inherent element in
the demand for political equality."[5]

The bloomer design used by Elizabeth Smith Miller could
have been based on practical styles of dress that she had seen in
use by her local Native American friends. During the early days
when women started using bloomers, Miller received praise for
her design of the bloomer. Lucy Stone and Susan B. Anthony

applauded it. Cady Stanton endorsed it in <u>The Lily</u> and wrote about Miller,

> "I had always thought that Sobriny [her reference to E.S. Miller] was sensitive to public sentiment; too much so, ever to strike out for herself a new path, unaided and alone. But of late the very spirit of her sire [Gerrit Smith] seems to have inspired her anew."[6]

Some liberal-minded men endorsed the bloomer costume in spite of criticism among colleagues. Smith did so, but only mildly. He felt that the new style did not go far enough in liberating women. Syracuse abolitionist Samuel J. May approved of it, and so did his colleague, James Caleb Jackson.

The gold star for approval must go to Miller's husband, Charles Dudley Miller. Frances D. Gage said of him,

> "No man went through the ordeal with the coolness and dogged determination of Charles Dudley Miller, escorting his wife and cousin [Cady Stanton] on long journeyings, at fashionable resorts, in New York and Washington [D.C.], to the vexation of all his gentlemen friends and acquaintances."

Cady Stanton noted of the critics,

> "the hostility of men… made it very uncomfortable for them to go anywhere with those who wore [bloomers]."[7]

The critics of bloomers accused women of attempting to end marriage and destroy the family by adopting trousers, which had always been a symbol of male authority. That some men were threatened by the introduction of bloomers actually exposed the weakness of their authoritative position in the face of women's demands for equality. But even so, the conservative power of cultural norms was difficult to overcome. Said Cady Stanton,

> "I wore the [bloomer style] two years and found it a great blessing…. Yet such is the tyranny of custom that to escape constant observation, criticism, ridicule, persecution, mobs, [I] went back to the old slavery [of long dresses] and sacrificed freedom…."[8]

The reason that she and other women's rights activists eventually rejected bloomers had more to do with the practical considerations of achieving their goals than with disagreeing in principle. They liked the change, but the price paid was too great. Cady Stanton enjoyed the freedom of activity they allowed, but not "the persistent persecution and petty annoyances suffered at every turn." She asked, "what is physical freedom compared with mental bondage?" She felt that "the martyrdom proved too much for us who had so many other measures to press on the public conscience."[9]

One of Cady Stanton's responses to the dilemma of what to wear was that clothing for men and women should be alike. Women, she said, "should dress just like man." This would afford women progress toward equality by reducing discrimination against them. One must ask, if identical clothing styles for men and women might lessen discrimination, then why did she not suggest that men dress like women? The answer, of course, is that she was aware of the intense prejudice against the feminization of men. This points to her awareness of the inferiority of feminine gender characteristics, and it makes one wonder why she did not focus on that as a source of unequal rights.[10]

For his part, Gerrit Smith disagreed with Cady Stanton's suggestion regarding eliminating "these distinctions in dress." She asked,

> "If nature has not made the sex so clearly defined as to
> be seen through any disguise, why should we make the
> difference so striking [with differing styles of clothes]?"

Smith responded that whereas bloomers may not be an ad-
equate solution to dress reform,

> "however much the dresses of the sexes should
> resemble each other, decency and virtue and <u>other
> considerations</u> require that they should be obviously
> distinguishable from each other." (emphasis added)[11]

This exchange between Cady Stanton and Smith points to
what was a culture-wide problem at the time—and may still be
today. Cady Stanton wondered why there should be distinctions
between the sexes in dress, and Smith pointed out the reasons.
His reference to "decency and virtue" is weak, for those quali-
ties are difficult to specify, and probably maintainable under any
style of dress. So "other considerations" are what is important to
him, and they emanate from his, and most other males', <u>intent to
discriminate</u> against women.

If both sexes looked alike, differentiation and discrimination would become difficult to carry out. There must be a
clear line of distinction between groups for discrimination to
be effective in maintaining superiority. That's why the color
line works so well for interracial discrimination. If there is any
confusion regarding who is a member of the inferior groups, the
process breaks down.

The bloomer experiment lasted only two or three years, with
most women giving it up because of their concern that it would
inhibit public acceptance of women's rights issues in general.
Elizabeth Smith Miller was the stalwart who wore bloomers

for seven years, including during her time in Washington, D.C. when Gerrit was there for his Congressional term.[12]

Cady Stanton eventually saw the bloomer episode as a diversionary failure in the pursuit of unity among women. Perhaps Frances D. Gage stated the issue most clearly in a letter to Frederick Douglass:

> "We must own ourselves under the law first—own our bodies, our earnings, our genius, and our consciences; then we shall turn to the lesser matter of what shall be the garniture of the body."[13]

Although the dress reform issue did not result in long-term physical change, it did attract much-needed attention to issues about which women had serious, deep-seated concerns--such as marriage and divorce.

EIGHT

Marriage and Divorce

"In the review of woman's position—of her profitless labor—of her crippling, dwarfing dress—of her civic and legal disabilities— of her religious bondage—of her social degradation—... those who... have borne the yoke of womanhood,... now clearly see that the most fatal step a woman can take... is... marriage...."
—Elizabeth Cady Stanton,
"Paper for the Yearly Meeting of the
Friends of Human Progress," 1857

Elizabeth Cady Stanton's opinion of the institution of marriage as it was constituted in the nineteenth century was cynical—and justifiably so. A combination of social customs and legal restrictions shackled women's liberty under the euphemistic guise of "protection." The marriage relationship was an intentional betrayal of woman's expectations of freedom in a republican nation.

In a letter to Susan B. Anthony, Cady Stanton howled, "it is in vain to look for the elevation of woman as long as she is degraded in marriage." And of Lucy Stone she asked, "How can she devotedly subscribe to a theology which makes her a conscientious victim of another's will...?"[1]

Cady Stanton's life's work revolved around a search for the causes of the subordination of women. Early on she focused on marriage as a cause, and later, on religion (see chapter 9). Her goal was to aid women's perceptions of themselves as dignified *persons* instead of as *subjects*. She was not sure that "the world is quite willing or ready to discuss the question of marriage…." She felt that the mid-nineteenth century might not be the right time for liberal reform ideas to influence that institution.

> "We have not yet outlived the old Feudal idea—the right of property in woman. The term marriage expresses the nature of the relation in which man alone is recognized. It comes from the Latin 'Maris', husband. Hence,… 'marital rights' [means] the rights of the husband…. I would have woman repudiate marriage utterly and absolutely, until our tyrants shall revise their canons and their codes."[2]

If marriage, she said, were to have one party dominate the other in an unequal contract, the dominant ought be the woman. "To… the mother of the race belongs the scepter and the crown." And this should apply worldwide, she argues. But such was not the case.

> "In all history… woman is regarded and spoken of simply as the toy of man,—made for his special use,— to meet his most gross and sensuous desires…."[3]

There was evidently much latent agreement among women regarding Cady Stanton's opinions about marriage. Her public lectures on the subject attracted more attention than did her presentations on other subjects. She called marriage a form of "instant civil death" that turned a potentially self-confident and self-sovereign woman into an "ignoble, servile cringing slave."[4]

In an ideal marriage, Cady Stanton believed, power between the two parties could be kept in balance. She had seen such relationships in Iroquois culture where shared duties and responsibilities, and an equal voice in decision making led to stability, and dominance by either party led to *in*stability. Perhaps the "Mother Earth" ecological lessons learned by the Native Americans had taught them the value of balance for human affairs also.

She saw little balance in marriage relationships around her, and believed that to be an important deficiency. Men could acquire a sense of mental balance from sources outside the home such as work, business, politics, religion, clubs, and recreation. But for a woman, domesticity was the focus of her daily experience, and tensions there could not be escaped. As she put it,

> "Marriage is not all of life to a man.... He has the whole world for his home, [and] his friendships with either sex, can help to fill up the void made by an unfortunate union or separation. But to woman, marriage is all and every thing; her sole object in life,—that for which she is educated,—the subject of all her sleeping and waking dreams."[5]

"In a true [marriage] relation," she said, "the chief object is the loving companionship of man and woman, their capacity for mutual help and happiness, and for the development of all that is noblest in each other." But, she lamented,

> "Marriage today, is in no way viewed as an equal partnership, intended for the equal advantage and happiness of both parties. Nearly every man feels that his wife is his property, whose first duty, under all circumstances, is to gratify his passions, without the least reference to her own health and happiness, or the welfare of their offspring; and so enfeebled is woman's judgment and moral sense from long abuse, that she believes so too, and quotes from the Bible to prove her own degradation."[6]

In sum, Cady Stanton saw marriage as a disadvantage for both parties because it crushed the 'better angels' of their nature. Humanity had evolved and survived due to its ability to cooperate, and western culture had designed in marriage a way to contradict that theme. She advocated a new view of marriage as simply a legal relationship that could be altered by either party, rather than an unalterable, sacred relationship.[7]

A fair question to ask at this point is, what was *her* marriage like? Shortly after Elizabeth Cady met Henry Stanton in Peterboro in October of 1839, she felt certain that her father would disapprove of her dream of marrying him. He did, and in her conflicted state, she postponed their marriage plans. But they did marry on May 1, 1840 in Johnstown, New York. Because of her dreams of an equitable marriage, Elizabeth insisted that the word "obey" be eliminated from her marriage vow. She latter quipped,

> "I think all these reverend gentlemen who insist on the word 'obey' in the marriage service should be removed for a clear violation of the Thirteenth Amendment to the Federal Constitution, which says there shall be neither slavery nor involuntary servitude within the United States."[8]

In spite of her hopes for an equitable marriage relationship, Henry treated her as a subordinate. "Marriage," she said, "is by no means an equal partnership…. A woman has no name!… She takes the name of her owner, [and this] is the symbol of the most cursed monopoly…." Henry was often away from home for long periods of time, and his freedom to be himself and chase his dreams angered Elizabeth.

> "As I contrast his freedom with my bondage and feel that,… I have been compelled to hold all my noblest aspirations in abeyance in order to be a wife, a mother,

a nurse, a cook, a household drudge, I am fired anew and long to pour forth from my own experience the whole long story of women's wrongs."[9]

Cady Stanton complained to Elizabeth Smith Miller, "how impatient I feel in my domestic bondage...." She wanted to accept invitations to travel and speak, but could not. She felt trapped. "How much I long to be free of housekeeping and children, so as to have time to think and read and write." She had seven children, and felt aggrieved that caring for them kept her from accomplishing her reform dreams. Just after the birth of her sixth child, Harriot Eaton Stanton, she wrote to Susan B. Anthony,

> "Oh how my soul died within me as I approached that dreadful, never-to-be-forgotten ordeal [of birth]....
> I am very happy that terrible ordeal is past.... I feel disappointed and sad at the same time at this grievous interruption of my plans. I might have been an orator...."[10]

After her childbearing years, Cady Stanton moved to Tenafly, New Jersey, just one hour by train from New York City. The move affirmed an unofficial separation of Elizabeth and Henry, and was symptomatic of her new sense of independence. She felt "vital forces" flowing toward her intellect instead of her womb. She was gearing up for reform activity. One aspect of discrimination that she had in her sights was the legal subordination of women.[11]

Laws that controlled the status of women in nineteenth-century America were grounded in English common law through Blackstone's "Commentaries on the Laws of England," which stated:

> "The very being or legal existence of the woman is suspended during the marriage, or at least is incorpo-

> rated and consolidated into that of the husband; under
> whose wing, protections and cover, she performs every
> thing."

At the point of marriage she became a <u>feme covert</u>, a woman
covered by her husband.[12]

Cady Stanton's philosophy of self-sovereignty asserted that the
natural rights of equality and independence should be extended
from the civic realm of politics to the private realm of domestic
relations, thus overturning feudal notions of loyalty, obedience,
and hierarchy. Self-sovereignty referred to the ability of a woman
to control her own life, and it rejected the notion of the male
having property rights to his wife. She viewed marriage as the
major force robbing women of legal identity and human rights.

> "Out[side] of marriage, woman asks nothing... but the
> elective franchise. It is only in marriage that she must
> demand her rights to person, children, property, wages,
> life, liberty, and the pursuit of happiness."[13]

Cady Stanton even challenged the contract status of a marriage. In order to be legally valid, she noted, a contract

> "must be formed between parties of mature age, with
> an honest intention in said parties to do what they
> agree.... But in marriage, no matter how much fraud
> and deception are practiced, nor how cruelly one or
> both parties have been misled,... the contract cannot
> be annulled.... [Women] live in legalized prostitu-
> tion!... held there by... the iron chain of the law."

And when institutions are supported by law, she claimed, the
only way of succeeding at overturning that law is "by revolution."[14]

The subject about which marriage law was most restrictive involved ownership of property. Polish-born women's rights activist Ernestine Rose moved to New York City in 1836. She advocated property rights for women as the necessary initial step in pursuing reform of women's status. When a women's property rights bill was first introduced in the New York State legislature by human rights advocate Thomas Hertell in 1836, Cady Stanton lobbied in favor of it. Between 1841 and 1848, eight bills for married women's property rights were introduced there, but none emerged from the committee discussion stage. Much of the support for such bills came from wealthy families that were worried about daughters losing title to property if they married.[15]

At the New York State Constitutional Convention of 1846, attendees refused to accept the idea that women should have the right to hold title to property. New York City delegate Charles O'Conor successfully argued that, "If there was any thing in our institutions that ought not to be touched by the stern hand of the reformer it was the sacred ordinance of marriage." Notice that he considered marriage to be a "sacred ordinance"—a law supported by religion—instead of a civil agreement as Cady Stanton advocated. The reason that reformers should not touch marriage, O'Conor continued, was that as the law stood, it "recognized the husband as the head of the household, merged in him the legal being of the wife so thoroughly, that in contemplation of law she could scarcely be said to exist."

Importantly, O'Conor referred to "the wife" as an object, a thing, as is "the household." The user of the reference "the wife" objectifies his partner in life, identifies her as a thing to be used, and reveals his intent to discriminate.

Interestingly, the same convention also considered and rejected the case for black suffrage. As a delegate, Gerrit Smith's former business clerk Federal Dana voted in favor of it.[16]

The married women's property bill that did become law in New York State in 1848 was the first such act in the nation, and, although it was cheered by women generally, Cady Stanton considered it to be "half a loaf." The law prohibited a husband from disposing of property brought into a marriage by a woman, but did not allow her contractual rights. The positive results of the law were that it brought radical women's rights literature into public view, and stimulated interest and activity for the pursuit of other rights for women, such as suffrage. In 1860, the original bill was amended to allow women to own property acquired through labor or inheritance, and entitled a woman to one-third of her husband's estate upon his death.[17]

Another legal issue associated with marriage was divorce. In the mid-nineteenth century, marriage was supposedly a covenant with God that no one had the right to dissolve. God was, and still is, considered to be male, thereby establishing a power base for the rule against breaking one's marriage vows. The power game played by those who consider the deity to be male is difficult for even some of the most liberal minds to perceive. Even Gerrit Smith never saw its sexist implications.[18]

Regarding bad relationships supposedly secured by religion, Cady Stanton asked, "Do you believe... that all these wretched matches are made in heaven? That all these sad, miserable people are bound together by God?" She thought it to be an absurd notion that some mystical power should bind together irrevocably the emotional states of two individuals who change over time. "Our present laws, our religious teachers, our social customs on the whole question of marriage and divorce, are most degrading to women," she wrote to her cousin Gerrit. She was livid over the fact that a woman fleeing an abusive marriage could be legally returned to her husband by force of police action, much like a fugitive slave could be returned to his or her owner.[19]

Early in her life, Cady Stanton had witnessed an abusive marriage. She became aware of the "wisdom of a liberal divorce law," and held in respect those women who "have dared to sunder the unholy ties of a joyless, loveless union." In <u>The Revolution</u> she wrote,

> "I rejoice over every slave that escapes from a discordant marriage [in which both parties] loathe and despise each other. Such marriages are a crime against both the individual and the state, the source of discord, disease, death, of weakness, imbecility, deformity and depravity…."[20]

When she lectured on divorce and marriage, many women told her of their personal troubles. "Slavery," she commented, "is nothing to those unclean marriages." Although she was assailed for her opinion on divorce, she persisted because she knew she was right: "My reason, my experience, my soul proclaim it."[21]

Her approach to the lecturing process was initially optimistic, and reminiscent of the moral suasion technique of the early abolitionists. She seemed to be naïve concerning the bias entrenched around marriage and divorce:

> "I had no thought of the persecution I was drawing down on myself for this attacking so venerable an institution. I was always courageous in saying what I saw to be true, for the simple reason that I never dreamed of opposition. What seemed to me to be right I thought must be equally plain to all other rational beings."

But she did draw fire from several sectors.[22]

In general, opponents of Cady Stanton's liberal stand on divorce believed it would weaken the family. They focused on restraints on men rather than liberation for women. Men, they thought, should uphold their contractual obligations to women rather than have women become as selfish and individualistic as men. The feeling was that marriage was designed to protect women, and easy divorce would encourage men to abandon them and leave them financially destitute. Many women opposed divorce because they felt it would threaten their status, reputation, and children. Even Lucy Stone opposed pursuing the issue because of its potential to detract support from the overall women's rights movement.[23]

Probably the most ironic opposition to women's rights came from abolitionists. For many of them, the concern for human rights did not extend to women. The abolitionists' point was that problems with marriage were as much their concern as women's, and so they should not be taken up at a convention for women only. At the invitation of William Lloyd Garrison, Cady Stanton spoke on May 8, 1860 to the annual meeting of the American Anti-Slavery Society. She reminded them that women also were slaves in need of emancipation. Their reaction was not cordial.

Three days later she addressed the Tenth National Women's Rights Convention, offering resolutions on marriage and divorce. Powerful Boston abolitionist Wendell Phillips opposed her and tried to keep her resolutions off the record because he did not consider divorce a proper topic for women to discuss. Susan B. Anthony replied, "he is a man and cannot put himself in the position of a wife; cannot feel what she does under the present marriage code."

Cady Stanton agreed. "With all his excellence and nobility Wendell Phillips is [only] a man." Liberal, reform-oriented women understood clearly that even the most liberal men could not conceive of themselves as women, and were thereby doomed to be selfish. Empathy with women was impossible.[24]

Perhaps the best example of this came through Cady Stanton's cousin, Gerrit.

By the late 1850s, Gerrit Smith was a seasoned reformer. He had wrestled over technique with William Lloyd Garrison; convinced Frederick Douglass to endorse politics; founded a third party that was about to elect a president; served part of a term in the United States Congress; given thousands of acres of land to poor blacks and whites; established a school for blacks, a home for destitute children, and a Free Church; spent thousands of hours traveling and speaking about slavery, temperance, and women's rights; operated a successful underground railroad station; funded and engaged the actions of John Brown; organized a conference to oppose the 1850 Fugitive Slave Bill; and so on.

Smith had been Elizabeth Cady Stanton's mentor, idol, and role model for three decades. He had introduced her to runaway slaves, Native Americans, abolitionists, evangelists, and her future husband, Henry. He had schooled her in radical human rights ideas, reform strategies and techniques, and the power of oppressive institutions. He had warned her to be self-sufficient, politically-minded, and fearless in stating her ideas. She had good reason to believe that her cousin, probably the most powerful human rights advocate in the nation, would eagerly support her desperate pleas for a liberal divorce policy that could aid oppressed women in escaping their "bondage".

She was wrong.

Gerrit's seemingly universal empathy for the "down-trodden" and oppressed victim of institutionalized prejudice could not shine through his veneer of protection for male superiority in matters of marriage and divorce. He asked, "Why should people marry?" His answer reflects the prejudicial cultural norms prevalent in the 1850s: "Because it is not good that the man should be alone." A man needs a "bosom friend to soothe and cheer and sustain him amid the sorrows and sufferings that await him." He showed no sensitivity to the similar needs of women.[25]

He was also insensitive regarding divorce. In the 1850s, most states allowed divorce on the grounds of cruelty, desertion, or adultery. New York State recognized only adultery as legitimate grounds for divorce. Smith's position was "that in no case should there be divorce…. [N]ot even adultery breaks the tie of marriage." He used his own marriage to exemplify his ideas. "My wife is incapable of becoming the wife of another so long as I live." He meant this, of course, in the philosophical sense that she *should* not do so.:

> "My crime may be such as to make it incompatible with her self-respect…. But she is never to cease from her efforts for my reformation, and she is never to put herself in such circumstances as would disable her from receiving me, should I return to her in penitence…. Christianity… would have the wife forgive her husband when he repents of his lying or theft, and it would… have her take him back to her arms when he has repented of his adultery."[26]

Smith was giving Ann orders about what she "should" do to ensure that "the wife" remained loyal to a disloyal husband. He never mentioned what the obligations of a loyal husband should be to a disloyal wife, probably because he believed that the husband should always be dominant. And it is interesting to note that this cluster of opinions on marriage and divorce occurred in the 1850s when Ann and Gerrit Smith were experiencing a "mid-life crisis" during which they both expressed doubts about the viability of their own marriage.

In poems written to one another, Gerrit wrote:
"This day makes two and thirty years

Since I this wondrous woman wed:
'Tis proved by my briney tears
I'de better kept my single bed."

And Ann wrote about Gerrit's anticipated homecoming following a trip:
"And thou wilt welcome once again
My offering poor, in which I'de fain
Express my love, but all in vain—
The future makes me sad."

When Elizabeth Cady Stanton noticed that Ann was traveling more and staying away from her Peterboro home for longer periods of time in the 1850s, she wrote:
"They were a pattern man + wife
And led a happy, loving life….
But now, 'they say,' Nancy's growing capricious
And Gerrit, dear soul, is quite unsuspicious."

The point is that even though Gerrit Smith was a liberal thinker, was married to a woman and had a young daughter, he could still not identify closely enough with women to demonstrate empathic reactions to their perspective on life. Were he and millions of other males able to shed the cultural burden of fear of feminine identity, perhaps women's rights would not have been an issue of contention for so long. But it was—and is—and Elizabeth Cady Stanton spent her life advocating what she hoped would be solutions to the problem.[27]

Her general philosophy regarding divorce was that it should be an option for both parties without recognizing guilt in either. "The true standpoint from which to view [divorce]," she said, "is individual sovereignty…. [This recognizes] the right of individual conscience and judgment." She felt that divorce ought to be a respectable choice when a married couple finds "themselves unsuited to each other, and incapable of making a happy home." Divorce should be a reasonable and acceptable solution to problems of incompatibility.[28]

Cady Stanton noted that the decision to marry is often made by young people who are inexperienced regarding relationships and eager to be on their own. "If, as at present, all can freely and thoughtlessly enter into the married state, they should be allowed to come as freely and thoughtfully out again." She believed that "...companionship and conscientious parenthood are the only true grounds for marriage.... In as much, then, as incompatibility of temper defeats the two great objects of marriage, it should be the primal cause of divorce."[29]

People should not, she argued, be required "to live together in the marriage relation in continual antagonism, indifference, disgust...." Women needed to develop the will to say that they "will no longer tolerate statutes that hold pure, virtuous women indissolubly bound to gross, vicious men...." The source of much of this "viciousness," she thought, was drunkenness.[30]

The mid-nineteenth century era was one of high stress for many people. A deep, long-term economic depression in the late 1830s and 1840s had demoralized many who lost jobs and became poor. New scientific discoveries were challenging old certainties. New religious beliefs emphasized the significance of the individual, making people feel adrift from previously secure moorings. As a defense, many—especially men—turned to alcohol. Cady Stanton advocated that chronic alcoholism should be grounds for divorce in order to protect women from abusive husbands.[31]

It was not unusual for reformers at the time to view the use of alcohol as a cause of social ills in general, and to believe that they could foster change by limiting its use. Both Cady Stanton and Gerrit Smith tried to move society toward accomplishment of justice and equality by encouraging temperance. Smith referred to the dram shop (bar) as "the great manufactory of incendiaries, madman and murderers," and he set for himself the goal of convincing people of the immorality of drinking beverages that contained alcohol. He was probably more optimistic about the chances for success than was Cady Stanton, and a bit less practical in his techniques.[32]

While Smith preached about drunkenness, Cady Stanton was testifying before the New York State Senate, establishing a power base in organizations, and speaking at temperance society meetings. In 1852, she and Susan B. Anthony helped form the New York State Women's Temperance Society to pursue women's rights in general, and liberal divorce laws in particular. "It is pitiful," she said, "to see how many excellent women are dragging out a weary existence in [relationships with drunken men] from mistaken ideas of duty." The state of Maine had in 1851 enacted legislation prohibiting the manufacture and sale of liquor, this lending credence to her claim that it could be accomplished. Women someday might not have to obey a man who was "a cowardly, mean tyrant, or a foul-mouthed bloated drunkard."[33]

Smith and Cady Stanton did not—probably *could* not—understand the psychological and physiological dynamics of addiction, so they were unable to foresee their eventual failure in the cause of temperance. But their commitment to the cause was admirable. Probably the most valuable insight to come from a study of the marriage/divorce issue involves the insensitivity of men to issues that concern women, and the corollary insight that this insensitivity is rooted in men's inability to conceive of themselves as women. Smith was proud that he could conceive of himself as "a colored man," a fact that intensified his work in the abolition movement. But he never mentioned a similar identity with women.

In a letter to him, Cady Stanton speculated about the perceptions of men regarding marriage and divorce:

> "Did he ever take in the idea that to the mother of the race, and to her alone, belonged the right to say when a new being should be brought into this world? Has he, in the gratification of his blind passions, ever paused to think whether it was with joy and gladness that she gave up ten or twenty years of the heyday of her existence to all the cares and sufferings of excessive maternity?"[34]

For most men, probably not. When the wife of Gerrit's brother-in-law James G. Birney died, Birney's two children lived with the Smiths in Peterboro for three years to relieve him of the burden of child-rearing. In all of his communications during that time, Gerrit wrote very little about it.

It was not his work.

NINE

Religion

*"All religions thus far have taught the leadership and superiority of man, the inferiority and subordination of woman….
History shows… that the moral degradation of woman is due more to theological superstitions than to all other influences together."*
—Elizabeth Cady Stanton
"Has Christianity Benefited Woman?" 1885.

Elizabeth Cady Stanton and Gerrit Smith both became disillusioned with religion as they aged. In their early lives, however, they had embraced it.

The young Elizabeth's family was Presbyterian. She remembered that on cold winter days, "we trudged along through the snow, foot-stoves in hand, to the cold hospitalities of the 'Lord's House,' there to be chilled to the very core by listening to sermons on 'predestination,' 'justification by faith,' and 'eternal damnation.'" And while she was young, she believed it.

During Elizabeth's stay at Emma Willard's school, evangelist Charles Grandison Finney visited and lectured. Elizabeth was "converted," she said, to the new religion of the Second Great Awakening. "I was one of the first victims," she claimed, although even then, she was confused about how to "repent and believe." As she looked back on it, she lamented,

"I can truly say,… that all the cares and anxieties, the
trials and disappointments of my whole life, are light,
when balanced with my sufferings in childhood and
youth from the theological dogmas which I sincerely
believed, and the gloom connected with everything
associated with the name of religion…. Thanks to a
vigorous constitution,… I was able to endure for years
the strain of these depressing influences…."[1]

As she grew older, she began to see the numbing effect religion had on critical thought. In 1841, her new friend Lucretia
Mott counseled her,

"It is lamentable that the simple and benign religion
of Jesus should be so encumbered with the creeds +
dogmas of sects—Its primitive beauty obscured by
these gloomy appendages of man."

In middle-age, Elizabeth remembered that "my reasoning
powers and common sense triumphed at last over my imagina-
tion" as she understood and welcomed the new tenets of logic
and science and escaped the "gloomy superstitions" of religion.
She became scornful toward Christianity and felt betrayed by
the discrimination against women that was a cornerstone of the
institution of religion.[2]

Gerrit Smith's parents were not highly religious people, so
his early years were not burdened with negative thoughts about
humanity as Elizabeth Cady's had been. In college between 1814
and 1818, Gerrit was a secular young man who enjoyed the "sin-
ful" endeavors of drinking alcohol and gambling. He showed
little interest in religion. But by 1826, a series of personal trag-
edies and a new acquaintance led him to the church.

Within a few months after his graduation from Hamilton

College, his mother Elizabeth Livingston Smith, and his first wife Wealtha Ann Backus, both died. Although he wanted to continue his studies to become an attorney, he could not because he was required to take over his retiring father's land sales business. In 1822, he married Ann Carroll Fitzhugh, the daughter of a former Maryland slaveholding family. She was deeply religious, and she begged Gerrit to join the Peterboro Presbyterian Church with her. As he faced increasingly complex issues, he found Christianity to be a ready source of solace. He joined the church in 1826.

During the 1820s, the fiery revivals of Finney's Second Great Awakening were sweeping across central New York State, part of a region that would later become known as the "Burned Over District." By 1830, the revival spirit had increased membership in Methodist churches by sevenfold, while Presbyterian church attendance quadrupled and Baptist and Congregational church congregations doubled.[3]

By the late 1830s, though, Smith had become disgusted with the proslavery stance of all Christian denominations, and he embarked on the establishment of an antislavery church that was free of any denominational identification. The "Free Church" founded in Peterboro in 1843 supported a mix of religion and politics and became a forum for the antislavery movement. Lecturers at its pulpit included John Brown, William Lloyd Garrison, Frederick Douglass, Elizabeth Cady Stanton, and, of course, Gerrit Smith.

It was either in 1846 or 1847 that Cady Stanton delivered a lecture there titled "Fear," outlining her move away from fear of God toward a more optimistic sense of self-empowerment. She understood by this time that people had created the institutions they lived with—including religion and its gods. She sensed that feeling controlled by those institutions alienated people from their own creation, made them subservient to those institutions, and disempowered the people. Smith came to a similar conclusion in the 1850s.[4]

It was during the decade of the 1850s that Smith faced a cluster of stressful issues and events that forced him to rethink long-held ideas. He and Ann were becoming increasingly alienated, and his son was rebelling. Health issues threatened his life. The economy was destabilized, and civil war seemed imminent. As new scientific findings and technology developed, he saw the old, static interpretations of life to be fruitless. He came to view the Bible as an errant and pernicious history book written by people trying to secure their own superior positions. It "is made the cover of slavery... and the authority for degrading women," he wrote.

He transposed learning about God from the Bible to learning about God through nature. His new "Religion of Reason" proposed that one should study natural ecosystems in order to view and learn about inherent stability. The natural world, he noticed, was always in balance. Each of its thousands of living and non-living parts were of equal value in maintaining that balance. If any one part—like people—tried to dominate the whole system for its own benefit, instability resulted. It was the diversity of all the parts that worked together to produce stability, and one could see this and understand it through reason.

It was just a short step, then, to transfer this reasoning to the human social system. Its diversity of parts consisted of different types of people. If any one type claimed superiority and tried to dominate others, instability or disorder would result. If all parts (types) were seen to be of equal value, respect and stability would result.

The purpose of Smith's "Religion of Reason" was to see God in nature through reason, thereby affirming the value of human rationality in understanding the world. People could then believe that God did not create nature—or the universe—but that people created God. That is, the balance and order seen in natural systems was not ordered by a deity, but evolved due to interaction among the parts. Before scientific observation, people assumed that the order was *created* by a supernatural force. But now, they could reasonably understand how that order was produced without reference to God. By that same pattern of reasoning, they could understand how to maintain social balance, order, or peace.

By thus debunking the absolute sovereignty of God in creating the earth and humans, Smith concluded that absolutes could not exist, and that in our pursuit of knowledge, we can only approximate certainty. Today, even the most exact sciences agree with this principle—that we can only know anything within limits of tolerance.[5]

What all this means is that as Cady Stanton and Smith matured, they both viewed religion as a hoax designed by people in power for the purpose of maintaining their superiority. Their friend and colleague Susan B. Anthony expressed well the secular opinions of many regarding interpretation of the Bible:

> "I distrust those people who know so well what God wants them to do, because I noticed it always coincides with their own desires."

Cady Stanton's orientation toward religion progressed from blind faith to analysis based in reason, and she recognized a similar progression of ideas in the Smiths.

> "Together they passed through every stage of theological experience, from the uncertain ground of superstition and speculation to the solid foundation of science and reason."[6]

Cady Stanton's review of the available literature about ancient history revealed to her that long ago women had been treated with respect and held a "leading, independent position... for ages...." She wrote,

> "It is worthy of note that our... ancestors seem to have had a higher idea of justice to woman than American men in the nineteenth century, professing to believe, as they do, in our republican principles of government."

Woman in ancient civilizations was portrayed "in all her native dignity, self-poised and self-supporting, her own head and hands her guidance and protection."[7]

Cady Stanton's review of the major world religions of her day concluded that they all "taught the headship and superiority of man, the inferiority and subordination of woman...."

Her friend Matilda Joslyn Gage stated the point clearly:

> "the laws, civil and social, each equally burdensome, are of church origin, and not until the church is destroyed will women be freed.... The prevailing religious idea in regard to women has been the basis of all their restrictions and degradation. It underlies political, legal, educational, industrial, and social disabilities...."[8]

Cady Stanton agreed:

> "To no form of religion was woman indebted for one impulse of freedom, as all [religions] alike have taught her inferiority and subjection.... Whatever heights of dignity and purity women have individually attained can in no way be attributed to the dogmas of their religion.... These dogmas are an insidious poison, sapping the vitality of our civilization, blighting woman, and, through her, paralyzing humanity."

And she believed that the Christian religion was one of the biggest offenders. "The Christian doctrine," she noted, "made woman mentally and physically the inferior of man, and lawfully in subjection to him."[9]

When the third National Women's Rights Convention met in Syracuse in 1852, Gerrit Smith was in attendance. This was one of the few times he participated actively in the women's rights movement. His cousin Elizabeth did not attend, but sent a letter to be read at the convention. In it, she took dead aim at the target that she believed to be the most powerful source of the degradation of women—the clergy.

When she spoke about the clergy, Cady Stanton's words were accusative, harsh, and cynical. She believed them to be woman's "most violent enemies... opposed to any change in woman's position." Her letter to the 1852 convention declared that the male leadership of the Christian church did all in its power to make woman's "bondage... more certain and lasting, her degradation more helpless and complete."

Calling clergymen "the most bitter outspoken enemies of women," Cady Stanton urged all women to withdraw from the church. She argued that these "dolorous saints" lacked "those sweet virtues of courtesy and charity that might best fit them for good works on earth...." And if they were really interested in doing good instead of hurting people, they should go upon graduation from seminary to Turkey to enlighten "the inmates of the Harems to a true sense of their present debasement and not as is [the] custom immediately enter our pulpits to tell us of his superiority to us 'weaker vessels.'"[10]

Her caustic criticism of the self-aggrandizing clergy attracted a lot of public attention, and she found support among her fellow female women's rights activists. When Matilda Joslyn Gage formed the Women's National Liberal Union to oppose religious oppression, she agreed with Cady Stanton's claim that Christianity was a "religious weapon [in] man's hand," and wrote that "hatred of women was the centerpiece of Christianity."

Gage charged:

> "The Christian Church is based upon... the theory
> that women brought sin and death into the world,
> and that therefore she was punished by being placed
> in a condition of inferiority to man.... That every
> Church is the enemy of liberty and progress and the
> chief means of enslaving woman's conscience and
> reason, and, therefore, as the first and most necessary
> step toward her emancipation, we should free her
> from the bondage of the Church.... I am as much
> as ever a believer in the <u>invisible</u> church—but <u>not</u> in
> this rotten thing known to the world as 'the Christian
> Church.'"[11]

In her loathing of Christianity, Gage rivalled Cady Stanton. Gage noted that religion justified

> "Slavery..., the destruction of learning; the oppression
> of science;... the denial of woman of a right to herself,
> her thought, her wages, her children, to a share in
> the government which rules her, to an equal part in
> religious institutions—all these... are parts of what is
> known as a Christian civilization."

Cady Stanton agreed:

> "Women would not live as they do now... in violation of every law of their being... if subordination to
> man had not been made... the cardinal point of their
> religious faith."[12]

In the face of such vitriolic criticism from educated and eloquent women, how did the clergy and the church respond? Usually, the women were either ignored or labeled eccentric, naïve, ungrateful critics of benevolent men. They were treated much the same as were the abolitionists—considered to be crazy and unaware of the value inherent in the way they were being treated. The establishment would rationalize that their subservient status was good for women because it recognized their inborn physical and social weaknesses and afforded them protection. It is not surprising that Cady Stanton called women "slaves."

After the 1852 women's rights convention in Syracuse, a nearby Auburn clergyman boasted that "no member of [his] congregation was tainted with the unholy doctrine of women's rights." Byron Sunderland, pastor of the Plymouth Congregational Church of Syracuse characterized the meeting as a "Bloomer Convention."

Cady Stanton wrote of a conservative minister who had criticized her liberal position: "In all my life I never did desire so to wring a man's neck as I did his." She probably had similar reactions to many men who practiced 'priestcraft' against women. She had a clear sense of the power such men wielded both individually and through their respected organizations. The General Association of Congregational Ministers of Massachusetts had previously issued a Pastoral Letter as a response to public reform work by women that stated,

> "The power of woman is her dependence, flowing from the consciousness of that weakness which God has given her for her protection…. But when she assumes the place and tone of man as a public reformer… she yields the power which God has given her for her protection, and her character becomes unnatural."[13]

Much to the dismay of Cady Stanton, many women approved of their subservient social position. They felt safe and unthreatened by the "protection" of males; they did not regard their legal status as a form of domination. Their conservative position of having all the rights they wanted legitimated the power of males, secured them in their dominant position, and sapped potential power from the women's rights movement. "So perverted," said Cady Stanton, "is the religious element in [woman's] nature, that with faith and works she is the chief support of the church and clergy, the very powers that make her emancipation impossible."

Even members of the Women's Christian Temperance Union figured that Christianity elevated the status of women by protecting them through the maintenance of male power. And when Antoinette L. Brown was ordained in 1853 as the first female graduate of Oberlin Theological Seminary, she softened the Christian subjection of women by blaming their inferiority not on religious teachings, but on sin. Her thinking was evidently mired in the cultural morés of the day that recognized the tradition of male dominance.[14]

In defense of equality between the sexes, Cady Stanton would at times call attention to the Biblical reference of Galatians 3:27-28, which recognizes the essential unity of all people. "For as many of you as have been baptized into Christ… there is neither male nor female: for ye are all one in Christ Jesus." But due to the power of the church in maintaining its standards, this usually fell on deaf Christian ears. Cady Stanton wrote,

> "So long as ministers stand up and tell us that as
> Christ is the head of the church, so is man the head of
> the woman, how are we to break the chains which have
> held women down through the ages?"

Susan B. Anthony also felt the power of Christianity. Speaking about acquiring the vote for women, she claimed, "The measure could be carried against all opposition if every clergyman in every community would urge the women of his congregation to work for it...."[15]

The feature of Christianity that really rankled Cady Stanton's mind was the paternalism that appealed to absolute moral standards to settle social issues instead of appealing to democratic political activity. And, she also saw that its conservative approach to controversial issues obscured and devalued the conflict and confrontation necessary to resolve differences in the social treatment of men and women. Because Cady Stanton became so radical and anti-clerical in the late 1800s, some women's rights activists rejected her leadership. But she did not mind because she felt that she was right, and that her duty was to agitate by means of speaking and writing until the public got the point.

It was the superb orator and abolitionist Wendell Phillips who noted that educated people "fail in republican duty" when they did not "lead in the agitation of the great social questions which stir and educate the age...." He continued:

> "The freer a nation becomes,... the more need of
> this... agitation. Parties and sects laden with the
> burden of securing their own success cannot afford to
> risk new ideas.... The agitator must [have] no party to
> save, no object but truth,—to tear a question open and
> riddle it with light."

Frederick Douglass made a similar recommendation to young people opting for social change: "Agitate! Agitate! Agitate!"[16]

And agitate Cady Stanton did, as did her cousin. Gerrit Smith wrote of the clergy as "superstitious disciples" who were "submissive" to a theology of "dread." Devout followers fell into the trap of allowing their creed to do "violence... to your reason, and... not daring to let your reason condemn your creed." He viewed ministers and priests as perpetrators of delusion with the effect of being "pernicious."[17]

Both Smith and Cady Stanton wished to develop a brand of religion based in reason. Smith's "Religion of Reason" was much like what Elizabeth wanted—a religion "in harmony with science, common sense and the experience of mankind in natural laws." Both ascribed to the secular trend to interpret the Bible as a historical document written by fallible people in a time that did not have science to rely on for explanations. Cady Stanton urged Bible readers to "read and reason for themselves" and not accept Biblical prescriptions for the subordination of women. She warned:

> "...when our bishops, archbishops, and ordained clergymen stand up in their pulpits and read selections from the Pentateuch with reverential voice, they make the women of their congregation believe that there really is some divine authority for their subjection."[18]

To answer this threat, Cady Stanton focused on the Bible as a major source of the subjugation of women. She noted that there are two stories of creation in Genesis. The second one in Genesis 2:21-25 is the story most people know. In it, woman is created from Adam's rib as an afterthought, and is considered to be inferior. Elizabeth suggested that this second story was added by some "wily writer" in an attempt to legitimate male domination, because the first story of creation in Genesis 1:26-28 establishes equality of the sexes. In fact, the passage states that "male and female" were created simultaneously in the "image of God," thereby affirming the nature of God to be of dual sexuality. This point is of interest because neither Smith nor Cady Stanton understood the power game being played by referring to God as "He."

As a reactionary move, Cady Stanton began work in the late 1880s on "The Woman's Bible." She described it as an effort "to collect every biblical reference to women in one small compact volume [in order to] ascertain what the status of woman really was under the Jewish and Christian religion." When published in two parts in 1895 and 1898, it was a radical feminist commentary on the traditional Bible in which she explored the domination of women legitimated by Christianity, and tried to counteract its organized sexism. Her secular interpretation made it clear that she rejected the divinity of Jesus, whom she described simply as a successful political radical.

She also rejected the concept of the immaculate conception by Mary. In "The Woman's Bible," the original Bible was attacked for having obstructed women's progress toward equality. It was a point with which Lucretia Mott agreed, calling the centuries-old version "a giant scarecrow across the pathway of human progression."[19]

"The Woman's Bible" was translated into several languages. It was condemned by leaders of religion all over the world. Most women's organizations in the United States disapproved of it, some even calling it heretical. Cady Stanton's rejection of established Christianity as an impediment to reform was shared by the abolitionists during their work to emancipate slaves.[20]

Although the separation of religion and politics was the accepted rule, abolitionists countered it with the establishment of Free Churches in many local communities. These churches melded religion with politics through the operation of the Liberty Party, and they became a forum for messages about the abolition of slavery.

The Free Churches were established because all of the denominations of Christianity were, to some degree, proslavery.

The more radical abolitionists like Smith could not condone participating in them. He said of the people in his local churches,

> "The Presbyterian and Baptist Churches of Peterboro would discipline one of their members who should vote for a sheep thief—but not if he should vote for a man thief (slave owner)."

Cady Stanton objected to the traditional church because of its proslavery and anti-woman positions. She wrote "The Slaves Appeal" to give voice to the oppressed bondsman, saying, "Bow down neither to cotton or gold; to union, constitution, or law; to false judges or fawning priests; but in thy brother man behold thy God." She indicated here her understanding of the social origin of the institution of religion.[21]

Regarding women who were discriminated against by the church she asked,

> "Is the bondage of the priest-ridden less galling than that of the slave...? Priests at the alter discourse most lovingly of her holy mission to cook him meat, and bear him children, and minister to his sickly lust."[22]

Some of the Protestant denominations split due to factional stands regarding slavery. A church's stand on slavery usually depended on its doctrine regarding the source of power: if the church had a hierarchical organizational structure with God in control through priests or ministers, it tended to be proslavery. If the pattern was egalitarian, like the Quakers, then it tended to be more antislavery.

An example of a split based on these considerations was the case of the Methodists. In the 1770s, the strongly hierarchical Methodist Episcopal Church spawned a more egalitarian faction led by John Wesley. The Wesleyan Methodists welcomed reform and hosted both antislavery and women's rights activity in the 1800s. This attracted black ministers like Richard Allen, who believed that African Americans should be organized into a powerful pro-freedom Christian constituency. Toward that goal, he founded the African Methodist Episcopal Church in 1816, which within ten years had over ten thousand "adherents."[23]

The AME Church arose from and was "dedicated to social protest." It pursued antislavery work and allowed women into its pulpit. Its ideological base was the pursuit of social justice, whereas the older Methodist Church was ideologically based around the individual's quest for salvation. Clearly, the abolitionists' most vital connection to religion was, ironically, through their own efforts to establish churches that were sympathetic to issues of human rights.[24]

Both Cady Stanton and Smith chose to reform these entrenched and power-laden issues by studying the existing institutional system and working within it. Neither advocated dropping out to form a new and more perfect society; they instead held optimism in progressive thought that compelled them into crusades for achieving implementation of the human rights they knew everyone deserved. But in order to help *everyone* to achieve an understanding of the institutional system in which they lived, the system itself must be debunked. That is, for reform to work, the general public would need to shed its perceptions of institutions such as the church and the government as 'holy' or 'regal'.

Both Cady Stanton and Smith understood the human origins of all social institutions, and they believed in their ability to change them. As Elizabeth had said, people did not need to sacrifice agency and liberty to restrictive demands of institutions of their own creation. She wrote,

> "When women understand that governments and religions are human inventions; that Bibles, prayerbooks,

catechisms, and encyclical letters are all emanations
from the brain of man, they will no longer be oppressed by the injunctions that come to them with the
divine authority of 'Thus saith the Lord.'"[25]

'The Lord', they agreed, was the people themselves who had
invented the institution of religion. Therefore, "the people" held
the power to reinvent, or change, or *reform* that institution. But
how? As they matured, Gerrit Smith and Elizabeth Cady Stanton
saw that democratic political activity was the most appropriate
tool. It used institutions already in place, and was designed by
our own former revolutionaries to produce peaceful change.
Both realized that when formerly oppressed persons—women
or slaves—have property rights and become commercially valuable, they are treated with respect and recognized as having equal
rights with all other citizens in a democracy.

TEN

Politics

"People are beginning to inquire how far public sentiment should sanction or tolerate these unsexed women, who would step out from the true sphere of the mother, the wife, and the daughter, and taking upon themselves the duties and the business of men, stalk into the public gaze, and, by engaging in the politics, the rough controversies and trafficking of the world, upheave existing institutions, and overrun all the social relations of life."
—<u>Albany Register</u>, *March 7, 1854*

On February 14, 1854, Elizabeth Cady Stanton became the first woman to address the New York State Legislature. Her subject of "Women's Rights" elicited the above response from the editor of the <u>Albany Register</u>. He compared her speech with "the performances of… the clown in the circus,… or the minstrelsy of gentlemen with blackened faces…," and he chastised "feminine propagandists of women's rights" who seemed to be enjoying "the novelty of this new phase of hypocrisy and infidel fanatacism."[1]

This came, of course, from one who worried that women might actually gain power in political arenas, and threaten his own position of superiority. He had already had that fear reinforced when the 1848 National Liberty Convention met in June in Buffalo and actually cast votes for Lucretia Mott and Lydia

Maria Child as nominees for Vice President of the United States. As Wellman noted in her research, this was "the first time in U.S. history that a woman had been proposed for federal executive office."[2]

It made much sense in the mid 1800s for anyone who was interested in securing and protecting human rights to enter the political arena. It was the only chink in the institutional armor of male dominance. The church, the family, and the economy were all bastions of male power, impregnable to the arrows of female ire. Democratic politics at least offered the possibility of participation by women, even if only in relatively insignificant roles. Petition campaigns and antislavery fairs of the 1830s allowed women to get their feet in the door, and the support of some abolitionists encouraged further effort.

The blossoming of third parties in the 1840s inspired those with budding interest in women's rights to play the same game. Political parties at that time were effective vehicles for ideas. People read newspapers, flocked to listen to orators, and, due to the previous success of the Second Great Awakening, were receptive listeners with a fair degree of optimism and self-confidence. The political candidates of the era were less important as personalities than were the ideological themes they espoused. For example, during the 1830-1860 "Reform Era," every U.S. president supported slavery, and only one—Andrew Jackson—served more than one term.

As a radical abolitionist, Gerrit Smith would have nothing to do with the two major proslavery political parties of the time— Democrat and Whig. He realized the value and potential success of political activity, and he threw the full weight of his money and his reputation behind the formation of the Liberty Party in 1840. It was a one-issue party—the abolition of slavery—and the noise it made in national campaigns between 1840 and 1848 motivated enough like-minded members of other parties to coalesce into the liberal, human-rights-oriented Republican Party in 1854.

Smith's personal apolitical stand grew out of his isolation in Peterboro, his dedication to the crushing demands of his business, and his belief that successful politicians could seldom uphold moral principles. "Politicians," he wrote, "are apt to die poor—especially such of them as espouse principle." The power of public office, he believed, corrupted the office holders. "In the breasts of politicians," he wrote, "…ambition, the greed of gain and the lust of place and power have… much play."[3]

His reaction was to avoid political activity if he could, although constituents of his district often nominated him for public office. "I have never been in public life," he said, "and have no ambition—no disposition, whatever, to be in it." He realized that what he had learned during his life was "quite too scanty and piecemeal to serve me in situations, which call for the systematic studies and extensive knowledge of the statesman…." In spite of his opposition to their efforts, women campaigned for him when he was nominated as an independent for a seat in Congress in 1853. Cady Stanton wrote,

> "Antoinette Brown and Lucy Stone canvassed the twenty-second district to secure the election of the Hon. Gerrit Smith for Congress, and were successful in their efforts."[4]

Elizabeth's involvement in political activity came mainly through women's rights organizations. She spoke at conventions and legislatures, usually as a representative of a national association. Her introduction to political activity came through the antislavery movement in a very personal way. In 1840, her cousin Gerrit and her husband Henry were both deeply involved in antislavery politics, and Elizabeth watched and learned.

Gerrit helped organize the Liberty Party, eventually becoming its presidential nominee, and later splitting off to form the more broad-based Liberty League. Henry at first supported the Liberty Party and did battle in Boston with the apolitical moral suasionist William Lloyd Garrison.

It was in Boston that Elizabeth met Frederick Douglass. The two reformers inspired each other. She admired Douglass' incensed attitude toward slavery and dignified public manner, calling him "majestic in his wrath." When the Free Soil Party emerged in 1848, Henry supported its stand on the non-extension of slavery into western territories.

Other factors also encouraged Cady Stanton's interest in politics. The New York State Married Woman's Property Act became law in 1848. Even though it was a weak statement in support of women's rights, it was at least a beginning—and a reason for optimism regarding future action. In that same year, some Quakers led by Elizabeth's friend Lucretia Mott organized the Congregational Friends, a more liberal faction that supported women's rights and Free Soil, and became involved in political activity.[5]

As a symbolic act recognizing the importance of political action toward reform goals, Cady Stanton nominated herself in 1866 as a candidate for the House of Representatives from the eighth Congressional District of New York City. She wrote to the Electors of the Eighth Congressional District,

> "Although, by the Constitution of the State of New York, woman is denied the elective franchise, yet she is eligible to office; therefore I present myself to you as a candidate for Representative to Congress."

By the move, Cady Stanton intended to call attention to the issue of woman suffrage and to slap the wrists—or faces—of oppositional males. Ann Smith commended Cady Stanton for her bold move, and said that she wished she could vote for her. As an independent candidate, Cady Stanton received twenty-four votes. She certainly did not want or expect to be elected. Her opinion of politicians was much like that of cousin Gerrit: "Wily politicians," she said, "always have an eye to their personal aggrandizement,… and instead of grand measures based on principle, they [propose] partial measures based on policy…." The best politicians, she thought, would be people who were already recognized as leaders because they were morally principled and unselfish—like the abolitionists.[6]

Cady Stanton was also interested in the third-party concept. She noted in 1872 that both major parties were hopelessly outdated regarding women's rights. In spite of the fact that the Republican Party had been founded on the principle of human rights, its opposition to the extension of suffrage had convinced her that it was "petrifying rapidly," and she viewed the Democratic Party as being "in a state of decomposition…."[7]

When the call was issued for the May 1872 convention of the National Woman Suffrage Association, its literature read:

> "We believe the time has come for the formation of
> a new political party whose principles shall meet the
> issues of the hour, and represent equal rights for all….
> This convention will declare the platform of… The
> Republican party… has been false to its own definition
> of Republican Government, [and] the Democratic
> party… died in the attempt to sustain slavery…."

Believing the current state of political affairs to be moribund, Cady Stanton proposed that,

> "We therefore invite all citizens who believe in the
> idea of self-government [and] the reform of political

and social abuses... to join with us and inaugurate a political revolution...."

Following discussions during the convention, the women decided not to establish a new third party, but to encourage the Republican Party to include women's issues in its platform. The disappointing result as stated in the Republican platform:

"The Republican Party, mindful of its obligations to the loyal women of America... declares that her demands for additional rights should be treated with respectful consideration."[8]

Cady Stanton must have asked cynically, 'What additional rights?!' She and Smith both understood well that no government can grant rights; its proper function is to protect existing rights. The task for reformers was to enlighten the voting public as to what those natural and universal rights were, and to expect their unbiased support. And therein lies the problem: unbiased. The "voting public" was all male—and very protective of its power and superiority. The question of importance for women was, whom, and what, should they endorse?

This had been a problem for Elizabeth in the 1840s and early 1850s because Henry Stanton had aligned himself with the conservative and proslavery Democratic Party in an attempt to get a political appointment during the Pierce administration. To the dismay of both Cady Stanton and Smith, he had been elected as a Democrat to a seat in the New York State Senate in 1849. Smith even fought against Stanton's reelection in 1851, but he won anyway. Elizabeth was pleased—especially regarding her own public image—when Henry joined the new Republican Party in late 1855. She even traveled with him to support his efforts.

"I am rejoiced to say that Henry is heart and soul in

the Republican movement and is faithfully stumping the state once more. I have attended all the Republican meetings."[9]

In the summer of 1859, Cady Stanton wrote a letter "To the Women of the Empire State" in which she appealed to them to "demand" equal rights legislation. At this point in time she was still optimistic that Republican politicians would care enough about women's rights to actually do something favorable. She wrote,

> "We hope much from our Republican legislators…. We shall look for their hearty co-operation in every effort for the elevation of humanity."

But by the mid 1860s she had lost faith in the Republicans' ability to recognize women as citizens. She was disgusted with Lincoln's conduct of the Civil War, and she refused to support his reelection in 1864 because she did not want four more years of "heartless character or utter incapacity." By 1868, having watched the discriminatory policies of Andrew Johnson squelch any possibility of the success of postwar reconstruction, she was convinced that the Republicans' intent was to use their political power to establish a new caste system, and that "the Republican party [was] now near its last gasp."[10]

With the Civil War over, the late 1860s and beyond saw a resurgence of women's organizational activities, controversial appearances in public, and political agitation for the one right of citizenship that they believed would help them secure their power base and develop respect for them from other sectors of society: suffrage.

ELEVEN

Suffrage

"We are satisfied that public sentiment does not demand and would not sustain an innovation so revolutionary and sweeping, so openly at war with a distribution of duties and functions between the sexes,… and involving transformations so radical in social and domestic life [as woman suffrage]."

—Horace Greeley
Chair of the suffrage subcommittee of the
New York State Constitutional Convention, 1867

"After declaring [in the Declaration of Independence] 'that no just government can be formed without the consent of the governed,' 'that taxation without representation is tyranny,' it is difficult to see on what basis one-half of the people are disfranchised."

—Elizabeth Cady Stanton, 1898

When the Statue of Liberty was unveiled in the New York City harbor in 1886, women suffragists called it "a gigantic lie, a travesty, and a mockery…. It is the greatest sarcasm of the nineteenth century [to represent liberty as a woman] while not one single woman throughout the length and breadth of the Land is as yet in possession of political liberty."[1]

The battle over woman suffrage produced a major division between men and women, and it highlighted two fundamental issues: the right of an adult citizen of a democracy to vote, and the power of white males to prevent it. This contradiction was so evident in nineteenth-century America that Elizabeth Cady Stanton asked American political leaders,

"If serfdom, peasantry, and slavery have shattered kingdoms, deluged continents with blood, scattered republics like dust before the wind, and rent our own Union asunder, what kind of a government [can] American statesmen... build with the mothers of the race crouching at your feet, while... peasants, serfs, and slaves, exalted by your hands, tread our inalienable rights into the dust? While all men, everywhere, are rejoicing in new-found liberties, shall woman alone be denied the rights, privileges, and immunities of citizenship?"[2]

Cady Stanton's analytical mind and incisive perceptions could often see deeply into the underlying causes of social issues. She and Anthony and Gage wrote the preface to Volume III of the "History of Woman Suffrage," offering an intriguing psychological reason for the reluctance of men to support woman suffrage:

"The rulers in the State are not willing to share their power with a class equal if not superior to themselves, over which they could never hope for absolute control, and whose methods of government might in many respects differ from their own."

As selfish power mongers, she thought, men feared that women were smarter about governance, and could do a better job of it.[3]

Regarding the ability of one group of people to empathize with another, Cady Stanton said, "It is impossible for one class to appreciate the wrongs of another." She stated this as an absolute, and probably overdid her point that men in power have difficulty perceiving the intensity of humiliation felt by women who are disfranchised.

Using her cousin Gerrit, whom she perceived to be more empathic than most men, she said of his refusal to sign a petition in support of woman suffrage, "Men always judge more wisely of objective wrongs and oppressions, than of those in which they are themselves involved." And his level of involvement in this issue, she thought, hinged on the loss of male power. His empathy was overrun by prejudice and tradition in the case of women, but it was not the same for blacks. Smith's claim that he could personally feel the bondage of blacks moved him to support suffrage for them. Did he think there were no black women? If slavery had dehumanized black men and suffrage would empower *them*, why was it not the same for women? Because—as we have noted before—Smith could not think of himself as a woman.[4]

Gerrit Smith had built a "Religion of Reason" based on balance in the natural world. Why, then, could he not see the balance of woman's perspective as necessary to the stable governing of a nation? His "self-application" rule to judge the validity of law fails here. Would he consent to wait for someone else to grant him his right to vote? In essence, Cady Stanton's argument had Smith "pinned to the wall," clearly revealing an inner conflict created by his long-standing support of inherent rights and his inability to conceive of himself as a woman. Smith illustrated the dilemma faced by many abolitionists, thus exposing a deeply entrenched cultural prejudice against women.

African-American men and women generally felt no contradiction in supporting woman suffrage, and they challenged white men to welcome feminism into their own lives, thus transforming their attitudes toward women. But that effort was doomed by the intensity of anti-woman prejudice supported through the church, the home, and the economy. Cady Stanton expressed her frustration in a letter to Lucretia Mott:

> "Our demands at the first seemed so rational that I thought the mere statement of woman's wrongs would bring immediate redress. I thought an appeal to the reason and conscience of men against the unjust and unequal laws for women that disgraced our statue books, must settle the question. But I soon found, while no attempt was made to answer our arguments, that an opposition, bitter, malignant, and persevering, rooted in custom and prejudice, grew stronger with every new demand made, with every new privilege granted."[5]

Her attitude sounds much like that of the moral-suasionist Garrisonians, who thought that pointing out the sin of slavery would lead to its abolition. Her frustration led to a bitterly ascriptive attitude toward others. The seed for the growth of what became her racist thought was planted in the post-Civil War effort to enfranchise black males.

As early as 1821, the chairman of the committee on suffrage at the New York State Constitutional Convention described blacks as

> "... a peculiar people, incapable... of exercising that privilege [of voting] with any sort of discretion, prudence, or independence. They have no just conceptions of liberty."

This early attitude made the point clear that it was legitimate to exclude some groups from voting in a democracy. Even though by 1804 every northern state had enacted measures to abolish slavery, the right of suffrage was restricted *by* white males *to* white males. This same attitude persisted even after limited emancipation in 1863, and after the total abolition of slavery in 1865. Between 1865 and 1870, when the Fifteenth Amendment enfranchising black males was ratified, a bitter division erupted between women and white males regarding the right to vote.[6]

When President Lincoln was assassinated in April of 1865, it became unclear who would provide political leadership for the coming era of national reconstruction. Congress was controlled by the ascending Republican Party, which was in turn controlled by the influence of former abolitionists who wanted to secure their power by achieving black male suffrage. But to do so, they needed to avoid the pending issue of woman suffrage; it was too divisive for the Republican Party to discuss it and maintain unity.

The newly recognized leader of the abolitionist faction was Wendell Phillips, whose position was that to pursue both black male and woman suffrage simultaneously would risk political power for the Republicans. "This hour," he said, "belongs to the Negro…. I say, one question at a time."[7]

The radical women activists thought this attitude to be typical of men, whom the women supposed normally had difficulty multi-tasking. The women responded by forming the American Equal Rights Association in May of 1866 to unite abolitionists and women's rights activists in one organization designed to pursue the common goal of universal suffrage.

Phillips turned down Lucy Stone's appeal to have the American Anti-Slavery Society merge with AERA, because he felt it would dilute the effort to acquire black male suffrage. The two causes, he said, "were not equally ripe."

The Fourteenth Amendment requiring equal protection of the laws was passed by Congress and submitted to the states for ratification in June of 1866, but it did not specifically include suffrage for either black males or for women. The Philadelphia Female Anti-Slavery Society declared that "the country and the Government belong to the white man; and [others may be] disposed of, in such a manner as may best serve the fancied interests of the white race." It seemed that allying with white, Republican males was what conferred power, so alienating them would prevent the achievement of any political goals. So thought men like Wendell Phillips, and even Frederick Douglass and Gerrit Smith. They reasoned that with Republican political power, black male suffrage could be achieved, and with that added political base, woman suffrage could be pursued. They did not want to commit political suicide by supporting woman suffrage too early.[8]

Just after the Civil War, Douglass sided with women regarding suffrage, but he changed his mind when he felt that both groups could not achieve it at the same time because of the lack of widespread public support. Black males, he thought, would have a better chance of acquiring the vote at that time because of whites' favorable opinion of blacks' contributions to the war effort. When women objected, Douglass justified his stand by claiming that blacks had suffered worse oppression than had females, and therefore deserved prior remedy. He suggested that women "hold their claims [to suffrage] in abeyance" until the black males had succeeded. His strange and ironic suggestion was that some oppression was to be condoned due to its lesser severity. As Douglass stated it:

> "I must say that I do not see how any one can pretend that there is the same urgency in giving the ballot to woman as to the negro. With us, the matter is a question of life and death, at least, in fifteen States of the Union. When women, because they are women, are hunted down through the cities of New York and New

Orleans; when they are dragged from their houses and hung upon lamp-posts; when their children are torn from their arms, and their brains dashed out upon the pavement; when they are objects of insult and outrage at every turn; when they are in danger of having their homes burnt down over their heads; when their children are not allowed to enter schools; then they will have an urgency to obtain the ballot equal to our own."[9]

Gerrit Smith held a similar opinion. He had written to Susan B. Anthony, "The removal of the political disabilities of race is my first desire, of sex, my second." He could see, and, he claimed, even *feel*, prejudice against blacks. Yet he seemed to have difficulty according the same emotions to women. "What fools their pride and prejudice make of [people]," he said. "[In] our whole... population... the spirit of caste prevails.... It is a mean, and hateful, and devilish spirit. It darkens and dwarfs... understanding." Smith did not get Cady Stanton's point that such a statement was as valid for women as it was for blacks. "Why is it," Smith asked, "that we are so especially slow to accord his rights to the negro? Is it because we are especially prejudiced against him? The degradation and disgrace of slavery are reflected upon him."

Cady Stanton pointed out to him that women were "slaves" also; that they were stereotyped as "servants" to "tyrannical" men. Smith had written a poem in 1865 exposing his stereotypical woman. He wrote to his friend Alida Littlejohn:

"The Standard Woman
To be a woman, noble, good,
Is what indeed each woman would:
To be 'The Standard Woman!' Oh!
Who's so ambitious that you know?

I know but one, Alida she
Who dares 'The Standard Woman' be
We heard her say 'by me' 'by me'
'Shall every woman measured be'!"

Littlejohn answered him derisively as follows:
"In those we love best we are often deceived
And even last night I could scarce have believed
That friend Gerrit who talks of 'Woman's right'
Could slander woman before it was light....
So wearily he tossed on his sleepless bed
'Till slanderous rhymes came into his head
Then calmly he slept till morning light
Then rose and girded himself for the fight
No more will I wrestle for woman's right
But down with her! Down! With all man's might!
Now all who may these simple lines see
I ask can Gerrit an honest man be
No! Hard and dishonest I'll proclaim him now
And forever and ever I will keep this vow!"

Smith's "Standard Woman" obscured his view of women as people with equal rights when it came to the franchise. He seemed stuck on the idea of men as the only valid voters. He told the New York State legislature,

> "...suffrage is a natural and inherent right. From the fact, that the province of Government is to protect person and property, it follows irresistibly, that every man has the right to participate in choosing the officers of Government... who are to wield the powers of Government for the protection of person and

property…. Wherever *his* home is, there has a person the right to vote."

Here Smith considers "persons" to be males, thereby disfranchising females.[10]

At the time when Gerrit Smith and Frederick Douglass were opposing woman suffrage, they were blinded by the hope that the influence of black males voting in the future would make it more likely that women would be enfranchised. Cady Stanton realized that enabling more men going to the polls would only solidify their dominance. She reasoned that women should attempt to "coattail" with black males to achieve the vote. "Would it not be wiser," she asked, "to… avail ourselves of the strong arm and blue uniform of the black soldier to walk in by his side?" In her typically practical thought, she wanted to use the black male as a tool to achieve her own political goals.

Former slave Parker Pillsbury had pointed out in 1865 that, because of continued discrimination against blacks, some northern states that had enfranchised black males had only succeeded in making him a "free nigger," and Cady Stanton worried that the same result might occur for women.[11]

It was the post-war issue of black male suffrage versus woman suffrage that led to a chasm between former allies in the crusade for human rights. Whereas former giants in the antislavery movement like William Lloyd Garrison, Wendell Phillips, and Gerrit Smith saw the need to focus on one issue at a time, radical women like Lucretia Mott and Elizabeth Cady Stanton saw a bigger picture of suffrage for all. Cady Stanton noted that reformers should "not talk of Negroes or women, but of citizens."

When the American Equal Rights Association was formed by women to pursue universal suffrage, it proposed in its preamble to "bury the black man and the woman in the citizen…."[12]

It was during this post-war era that the radical human rights activists changed from the male abolitionists to the emerging women's rights activists like Cady Stanton, Anthony, and Mott. And as the rift between these two groups grew, disagreements between them became personal as well as topical. Women felt deceived and betrayed by men who had fought only until they got what they wanted for themselves: more male power. Cady Stanton remarked that at that moment, "The women generally awoke to their duty to themselves.... If the leaders in the Republican and abolition camps could deceive us, whom could we trust?" She noted years later that their promises to support woman suffrage were "still unredeemed."[13]

In January of 1867, Cady Stanton addressed the New York State Legislature and warned them not to listen to the minority of women who opposed the extension of suffrage. "Remember the gay and fashionable throng who whisper in the ears of statesmen... 'We have all the rights we want,' are but the mummies of civilization...." Later that spring, the state Constitutional Convention Committee on Suffrage refused to support woman suffrage, and it was defeated by a lopsided vote of 125 to 19. Male legislators generally believed that women were not oppressed, that most women did not want to vote, that suffrage was pursued only by a few women who were seeking notoriety, and that women voting would split homes. Such prejudiced opinions led radical women to attack patriarchy.[14]

Cady Stanton noted that nations built on caste systems had failed, so "Why in this hour of reconstruction, with the experience of generations before us, make another experiment in the same direction?" The woman's vote was needed, she said, because

> "The male element is a destructive force, stern, selfish,
> aggrandizing, loving war, violence, conquest, acquisi-

tion, breeding in the material and moral world alike discord, disorder, disease, and death."

Male rulers in the home and in politics, she maintained, approved of women as long as they were quiet and subservient. But when a woman dared to demand her rights, she became intolerable. William Lloyd Garrison labeled Cady Stanton as "untruthful, unscrupulous, and selfishly ambitious." Other former abolitionists also slapped her wrist for being assertive.[15]

That assertiveness had grown out of her frustration with reformers who claimed to run their lives on moral principle, but failed to apply it to issues that concerned women. No wonder she felt betrayed! She proclaimed that the abolitionists had forgotten the "well learned lesson taught in the early days of anti-slavery… that all compromises with principle are dangerous."

As an example, Cady Stanton used her cousin Gerrit, who had said just after the war in 1865, "Am I asked whether I would have all men vote? I answer that… I would—and all women too." But later, he changed his stand: "Very desirous am I that justice be done to woman…. But my first duty is to my colored brothers and sisters."[16]

Why, Cady Stanton wanted to know, were there "firsts" and "seconds" in principle? Why could he—and others—feel so clearly the post-war discrimination against blacks, but not that against women? She charged,

> "Mr. Smith abandons the principle clearly involved….
> Even such just and liberal men as Gerrit Smith and
> Wendell Phillips… lost sight of the ever-binding
> principles of justice…."[17]

Susan B. Anthony also appealed to Gerrit Smith's principled stand in the hope of acquiring his support for woman suffrage. She asked,

"To whom shall our Equal Rights work look if not to you at this hour of its great need…? You will hear my appeals to you, Mr. Smith, I know—for your love for the principles of *equal* rights to *all* is never failing."

Yet he refused her request to sign a petition for woman suffrage because he feared that doing so would work "against the enfranchisement of the negro man…."[18]

Cady Stanton criticized Smith for making the issue too complicated. "You have now to right yourself on the social questions. To your mind [woman suffrage is] a tough and tangled problem. To mine, as simple as those you have already solved." She advised him to follow his own long-held principles, and "the facts of life and the deductions of logic [will] drive you irresistible to my ground." She had not lost all faith in Smith's ability to be empathic, but she was greatly disappointed in him at this time. As she put it,

> "…in criticising such good and noble men as Gerrit Smith and Wendell Phillips for their apathy on woman's enfranchisement at this hour, it is not because we think their course at all remarkable, nor that we have the least hope of influencing them, but simply to rouse the women of the country to the fact that they must not look to these men as their champions at this hour. While philosophy and science alike point to woman as the new power destined to redeem the world, how can Mr. Smith fail to see that it is just this we need to restore honor and virtue in the Government? There is sex in spiritual as well as the physical, and what we need to-day in government, in the world of morals and thought, is the recognition of the feminine element, as it is this alone that can hold the masculine in check."[19]

Because of Smith's inability to identify himself as a woman, he saw Cady Stanton's criticism of him as being out of tune with reality. But she thought the same of him. Which side one agreed with depended on whose "reality" one accepted. Smith focused on the policy-based reality of the movement that woman suffrage was so unpopular an idea that it had no chance of being achieved. Cady Stanton focused on the principle-based reality of the universality of human rights. But it was the white males who held the political power, and they chose to ignore women. Cady Stanton saw this clearly.

In 1868 Elizabeth Smith Miller, Susan B. Anthony, Elizabeth Cady Stanton, and Abby Hopper Gibbons (daughter of abolitionist Isaac Hopper) sent a letter to the National Republican Convention in Chicago, asking that the party recognize the right of woman suffrage in its platform. The letter was ignored. When Lucretia Mott died, Cady Stanton wondered, "Why are the press and the pulpit, with all their eulogisms of her virtues, so oblivious to the humiliating fact of her disfranchisement?"

Being ignored by most men and many conservative women made the women's rights advocates wonder if they would ever succeed. Cady Stanton lamented that with

> "their long-time friends against them; such as Charles Sumner and Henry Wilson in the Senate, William Lloyd Garrison and Gerrit Smith in reform, Horace Greeley and most of the liberals in the press, the position of women seemed so untenable to the majority that at times a sense of utter lonliness and desertion made the bravest of them doubt the possibility of maintaining the struggle or making themselves fairly understood."[20]

Even the most liberal human rights advocates of the era, said Cady Stanton, failed to perceive the degradation felt by women:

"Gerrit Smith… does not clearly read the signs of the
times, or he would see that there is to be no reconstruction of this nation, except on the basis of universal suffrage as the natural, inalienable right of every citizen.…
As the aristocracy in this country is the 'male sex,' and
Mr. Smith belongs to the privileged order, he… considers it important for the best interests of the nation, that
every type and shade of degraded, ignorant manhood
should be enfranchised, before even the higher classes
of womanhood should be admitted to the polls."

Frederick Douglass would not support woman suffrage along
with black male suffrage because, he claimed, women are loved,
but "the Negro is loathed," and therefore needed the vote for self-
protection more so than women. Douglass believed that women
were adequately enfranchised—even if vicariously so—through
males, and in that sense, were already politically empowered.
Black males lacked this indirect empowerment, he argued, so
they deserved the vote first.[21]

Immediately after the war, the political status of black males
was seen as a highly important issue by abolitionists and Republicans. They felt that black males were going to need to be enfranchised if they were to have the power to resist virtual slavery,
yet they could not perceive the same need for women. When the
American Equal Rights Association was formed by women in
1866 to support universal suffrage, their initial petition asserted
that

"Women and the colored man are loyal, patriotic,
property-holding, tax paying, liberty-loving citizens,
and we cannot believe that our sex or complexion
should be any ground for civil or political degradation."

But by 1869 the leadership of the AERA had been taken over by white males, who guided its support toward the enfranchisement of black males. Cady Stanton and Anthony dropped out to form the National Woman Suffrage Assocation.[22]

Women felt that they deserved the attention of the reconstruction era policy-makers, but could not get it. "Abolitionists," said Cady Stanton, "have demanded suffrage for women for the last ten years, and why do they ignore the question now?" How could women, she wondered, deserve less than the soldiers who fought in the war? Why did not the contributions and sacrifices of women during the war open the eyes of abolitionists to their equal status in the fight for suffrage? During the war,

> "the patriotism of women shone forth as fervently and spontaneously as did that of man; and her self-sacrifice and devotion were displayed in as many varied fields of action…. The labor women accomplished, the hardships they endured,… can never be fully appreciated."[23]

Those who agitated for woman suffrage in the 1860s knew that if they did not succeed, their window of opportunity would be lost for a long time. Writing in retrospect, Cady Stanton noted:

> "Time has proved their fears well grounded. Nearly twenty years have passed, and there has been no such agitation and excitement as then on the question. If all the women, to say nothing of the Republicans and Abolitionists who claimed to believe in the truth of the idea, had stood firm, woman would have been enfranchised with the negro. But few could withstand the persecution, the ridicule, the pathetic appeals to keep silent, and in a large measure when the Anti-Slavery Society disbanded the woman suffrage movement became the toy of the Republican party, and has been

trifled with ever since, like the cat with the mouse in the fable."

Feeling frustrated and abandoned, women realized that they could not depend on men for support. The fight for suffrage would be their own. By the late 1860s, they knew that "reform" would not be enough. It would require a revolution in thinking. So when Cady Stanton and Anthony founded the radical feminist newspaper The Revolution in 1868, they stated that "we especially desire that The Revolution shall be the mouth piece for women."[24]

One of the unfortunate but understandable symptoms of frustration exhibited by Elizabeth Cady Stanton was her devaluation of other people who *were* enfranchised—especially the black male. Her outrage over the extension of suffrage to more males emerged as elitism and racism. She had been an abolitionist, but her reaction to the defection of former colleagues from the woman suffrage cause resulted in anger opportunistically projected onto the black man. This episodic outburst laid bare a latent racism that was not unusual at the time, even for the most liberal of human rights advocates. Her logical and practical thought led her to use the inferiority of some segments of society to support her own perspective on the urgency of woman suffrage.

Like her cousin Gerrit, her practical thought led her to switch tools when a task could not be achieved. When her original emphasis on universal human rights did not soften the bias against woman suffrage, she adopted the "moral leadership of women" stand, claiming that women's reputation for being more moral than men was a sign that they would make balanced decisions if they could vote. When the conservative political environment did not accept that argument, she resorted to ascriptive tools, labeling other groups as inferior to women.[25]

She developed an elitist argument concerning the superiority of women that emphasized their virtue and dignity above other groups. Women were a "higher order" of persons who should receive the highest priority for suffrage. Cady Stanton worked the elitist theme with skill, noting that women would "not feel so sorely aggrieved" if only men who had acquired the status of

> "Webster,... Clay, or Gerrit Smith could claim the right of the elective franchise, but to have the rights of drunkards, idiots, horse-racing, rum selling rowdies, ignorant foreigners, and silly boys recognized, whilst we ourselves are thrust out from all the rights that belong to citizens—is too grossly insulting to the dignity of woman to be longer quietly submitted to."[26]

She developed an especially vicious and arrogant attitude toward immigrants to the United States, whom she viewed as totally unprepared to exercise the vote. She suggested that

> "the best interest of the nation demands that we outweigh this incoming pauperism, ignorance and degradation with the wealth, education, and refinement of the women of the republic."

Of course, she meant *white* women. When criticized for her position, she responded, "We prefer Bridget and Dinah at the ballot box to Patrick and Sambo." She openly worried about the results of immigrants voting: "Think of Patrick and Sambo and Hans... making laws for Lydia Maria Child [and] Lucretia Mott...." She extended this elitism to white, female citizens of the United States. Of these women who accepted their non-voting status, she said,

> "That a majority of the women of the United States accept, without protest, the disabilities which grow

out of their disfranchisement is simply an evidence of
their ignorance and cowardice, while the minority who
demand a higher political status clearly prove their
superior intelligence and wisdom."

Gerrit Smith criticized her for holding an elitist position,
telling her that it denied the fundamental principle of universal
rights.[27]

Cady Stanton's reactionary stand carried obvious expressions
of racism. When she and Anthony established <u>The Revolution</u> in
1868, they did so with the financial backing of George Francis
Train, a "copperhead" Democrat. In that the Democratic Party
was proslavery, and copperheads were northerners who did not
support the Civil War, Cady Stanton and Anthony were openly
admitting latent racist tendencies. Cady Stanton's feeling of inferiority to black males led to her use of the derisive label "Sambo."
She stabbed at the white males in power, calling them

"the privileged order [who] look down complacently
and tell us, 'This is the negro's hour; do not clog his
way; do not embarrass the Republican party with any
new issue; be generous…; the negro once safe, the
woman comes next.'"

Cady Stanton was not ready to be told that she was "next,"
especially by those with power in the white boys' club. Her idea
was that when black males were enfranchised, women should

"press in through that constitutional door the moment
it is opened for the admission of Sambo [because]
self-preservation is the first law of nature."[28]

She was not convinced that black male suffrage would be of
any benefit to women. She worried that enfranchised black men

would be just as determined as white men to keep women from voting. "I would not trust him with all my rights," she admitted; "degraded, oppressed himself, he would be more despotic with the governing power than even our Saxon rulers are."[29]

Susan B. Anthony was quieter than Cady Stanton, but she still showed racist concerns. When black males did acquire the vote, she claimed that we have

> "lifted up two million black men and crowned them with the honor and dignity of citizenship, [and we] have dethroned *fifteen* million white women… and cast them under the heel of the lowest orders of manhood."

She did not mention black women at all, as if they were invisible.

Black women were well aware of their double jeopardy position regarding discrimination against them. Charlotte Forten, the granddaughter of successful Philadelphia African American businessman James Forten, complained,

> "Oh! it is hard to go through life… fearing with good reason to love and trust hardly any one whose skin is white— however lovable, attractive and congenial in seeming."

Her mother, Sarah Forten noted,

> "Even our professed friends have not yet rid themselves of [racism]. To some it clings like a dark mantle obscuring and choking up the avenues of higher and nobler sentiments."

Ann Smith once commented in a letter to Gerrit that the Fortens were visiting her in Philadelphia, and she hoped that they would leave before some of her white friends arrived.[30]

Sexist and racist intentions were actually codified into the United States Constitution. The original Constitution contained no reference to sex as a limit on the rights of suffrage, but when the Fourteenth Amendment was proposed by the Joint Committee on Reconstruction in April of 1866, it specified that only males would be subject to equal protection of the laws. This developed out of the post-war push to enfranchise black males. Cady Stanton called it an "attempt to turn the wheels of civilization backward," and she pleaded with cousin Gerrit for help:

> "If that word 'male' be inserted as now proposed... it will take us a century at least to get it out again. Oh! my cousin! Heal my bleeding heart with one trumpet note of manly indignation."

She knew that such indignation would pack more power if it came from a man, but her cousin did not respond.[31]

By 1871, Cady Stanton supported the notion that the wording of the Fourteenth Amendment gave all citizens the right to vote. But the United States Supreme Court negated that idea in 1874 by declaring that "suffrage was not 'co-extensive' with citizenship."[32]

The Fifteenth Amendment was also sexist. It prevented denial of the right to vote "on account of race, color, or previous condition of servitude," but did not include sex in that list. Cady Stanton revealed her disdain for the omission by quoting English philosopher John Stuart Mill. Such an act, he said, "constitutes every woman the inferior of every man... [and] declares every serf, peasant, and slave the rightful sovereigns of all womankind...." It is curious that she did not pick up on the idea that technically, it could be argued that women *could* vote because they were members of a "race." Susan B. Anthony even claimed that women could vote because being a wife constituted a "condition of servitude."[33]

Obviously, the issue of woman suffrage tilled such sensitive territorial turf that confrontation was inevitable. When Elizabeth Cady Stanton proposed at the 1848 Seneca Falls Women's Rights Convention that acquiring the vote was critical to the success of the women's rights movement, her husband Henry told her, "You ask for suffrage, and I'm leaving town." The intent of white males to prevent woman suffrage amounted to a self-inflicted injury to the whole society. The intentional crippling of women's political expression had alienated a majority of the population that had potential to become a socially subversive element. Cady Stanton once remarked that

> "The enfranchisement of woman is… to be carried by… constant agitation, and in new directions, attacking in turn every stronghold of the enemy…."[34]

The enemy, of course, was men. White males especially saw the woman suffrage movement, as Wagner so aptly states it, as "a radical and heretical challenge to the God-ordained authority of man." And in the mid-nineteenth century, that authority seemed well rooted. U.S. Senator William Henry Seward told Cady Stanton, "You have the argument, but custom and prejudice are against you, and they are stronger than truth and logic." By the post-war era, women knew this was true, and they understood that even if suffrage were gained, they would still face issues of discrimination. The end of slavery was no more the end of racism against blacks than acquiring the vote would be the end of sexism against women. Male monopoly on the proper interpretation of religious doctrine and the Bible reinforced the cultural domination of women, so getting the vote would not end oppression.[35]

The rationale for woman suffrage was stated clearly in the introduction to volume one of the "History of Woman Suffrage". Editors Cady Stanton, Anthony, and Gage wrote,

> "In an age when the wrongs of society are adjusted in the courts and at the ballot-box, material force yields to reason and majorities."

And when women could not express their reason or be counted, they felt aggrieved. The editors of volume four, Anthony and Ida Husted Harper, continued the theme of the significance of the vote.

> "This most valuable of all rights... is placed absolutely in the hands of men to be granted or withheld at will from women. This prejudicial, conservative and in a degree ignorant and vicious electorate [of men] possesses absolutely the power to withhold the suffrage from women."[36]

Cady Stanton's radical view of the importance of the vote alienated others who were more conservative. She saw it as "the point of attack, the stronghold of the fortress—the one woman will find most difficult to take—the one man will most reluctantly give up." Men claimed that having the vote was no big deal; that it was only one of a cluster of citizen rights in a democracy—and a minor one. Women, they claimed, focused on it because it was easily visible and quantifiable. Cady Stanton lashed back that the vote was

> "no shadow, but a substantive entity that the citizen can seize and hold for his [or her] own protection and his [or her] country's welfare. A direct power over one's own person and property, an individual opinion to be counted on all questions of public interest....

[I]ndividual sovereignty reveal[s] the beauty of representative government, and reveal[s] the beauty of united effort to carry a grand measure."

It is interesting to note her use of the male reference only. In spite of her radicalism, Cady Stanton was also "trapped" by lingering prejudicial custom.[37]

In their argument against woman suffrage, men claimed that women were naturally and fundamentally different from men, and were therefore unsuited for public/political life. Cady Stanton called them on this ruse to her own advantage by turning what seemed like a good argument for keeping women out of politics into a mandate for the vote: If women *were* so different from men, how could men effectively represent them? And if men could not legislate for them, then women needed to vote for themselves. But men believed that women would not do enough investigation of candidates and issues to be well-informed as voters. To that point, abolitionist and women's rights activist Sojourner Truth remarked,

"It doesn't seem hard work to vote…. Now, if you want me to get out of the world, you had better get the women votin' soon. I shan't go till I can do that."

Even though she was illiterate, Truth knew that the power of the vote went beyond the election of a candidate. As Cady Stanton put it,

"The ballot is the symbol of equality, and to recognize woman's equality in every position of life is to teach her self-respect [and] dignify her in the eyes of man…."

And if men perceived her as dignified, then many of the problems of female subservience could be solved. "There can be no subordination," she noted, "where the one to whom the command is given is allowed to sit in judgment on the character of the command."[38]

The tactics that women used to pursue suffrage varied over the decades, punctuated by a hiatus caused by the Civil War. English author Harriet Martineau commented on the powerlessness of women in her 1837 "Society in America." She wondered how "the political condition of women" could be reconciled with principles of liberty and sovereignty stated in the Declaration of Independence.

It was at about this same time that a nascent women's rights movement was appearing in the United States. The original tactic was public speeches by strong women associated with the antislavery movement. Quaker women like Sarah and Angelina Grimké and Lucretia Mott agitated in favor of power for women, and they became superb examples at the rostrum. Although they did not ask for the vote, their work attracted much public attention and initiated concern among women for their own status.[39]

At the May 1839 annual meeting of the American Anti-Slavery Society in New York City, a debate arose over the issue of women in attendance voting on organizational issues. The result presaged a split among abolitionists that would characterize the next two decades. Whereas William Lloyd Garrison, Gerrit Smith, and Theodore Dwight Weld approved of women voting, the more religiously based followers of Lewis Tappan opposed it. Their deeply Christian backgrounds prejudiced them against assertiveness on the part of women. This issue came to a head more clearly at the World Anti-Slavery Convention in London in 1840, when the British leadership refused to seat female delegates from the United States. Cady Stanton and Mott were two of those delegates who felt offended by the snub, and they resolved to hold a women's rights convention upon their return home. Cady Stanton wrote later that "The movement for woman's suffrage, both in England and America, may be dated from this World's Anti-Slavery Convention."[40]

An additional stimulus took place at the 1840 annual meeting of the American Anti-Slavery Society. When Abby Kelley won election to the business committee by a vote of 557 to 451, Lewis Tappan resigned and took his followers with him to establish that evening at his house the rival American and Foreign Anti-Slavery Society, which explicitly denied women the right to vote. As women participated in the antislavery movement in the 1830s and 1840s, they felt keenly the empowerment that came with a public role, and simultaneously, the disempowerment endured due to disfranchisement. The result was the fruition of Cady Stanton's and Mott's pledge to inaugurate a women's rights movement in the United States.[41]

It was at the Seneca Falls convention in July of 1848 that the first public demand for woman suffrage appeared. Resolution #9 of the Declaration of Sentiments read: "Resolved, that it is the duty of the women of this country to secure to themselves their sacred right to the elective franchise." Cady Stanton insisted on this political goal as part of the declaration—against the wishes of some of the participants. It was the only motion discussed at the convention that did not pass unanimously. Lucretia Mott opposed it, which shows how radical a proposal it was. It struck at the heart of male power, and even some of the most liberal women were wary of it.

Susan B. Anthony remarked, "It was almost the exact middle of the nineteenth century before the first demand was made by women for the right to represent themselves...."

Cady Stanton barked, "This right is ours. Have it was must. Use it we will...."[42]

In this antebellum era, the reaction of males was mixed. As a fledgling politician, Abraham Lincoln had supported suffrage for all whites who paid taxes; this distinction favored only a few women. Many abolitionists had adopted "feminine values" such as self-sacrifice and moral virtue, and were ready—at least before the war—to support woman suffrage.

In 1846, Syracuse abolitionist Samuel J. May had stated that "the disfranchisement of females is as unjust as the disfranchisement of the males would be." But not all those abolitionists who originally supported the women would stay loyal to their cause. Gerrit Smith serves as an example of a fluctuation of attitude toward woman suffrage that typified many liberal abolitionists.[43]

In June of 1848, just one month before the Seneca Falls convention, Smith supported a woman suffrage plan in the platform of the Liberty Party. In a speech at the Buffalo convention of the Liberty Party on June 14, 1848 he said,

> "This universal exclusion of women [from voting] argues, conclusively, that, not as yet, is there one nation so far emerged from barbarism... as to permit women to rise up to the... level of the human family. It also argues... that Civil Government... is... so unhappily confounded with these flagrant forms of injustice... as to make the thought of woman's participation in it revolting and absurd."

The plank for women called for "universal suffrage in its broadest sense, females as well as males being entitled to vote."[44]

Smith continued to support woman suffrage throughout the 1850s. At the September 1852 Liberty League Convention in Canastota, he held "that all persons—black and white, male and female—have equal political rights, and are equally entitled to the protection and advantages of Civil Government." And he repeated the same idea in a June, 1857 speech in Milwaukee.

Grateful for his support, Cady Stanton told him, "I have never felt… disappointment in the sage of Peterboro." That opinion was about to change.[45]

That change, however, would wait until after the Civil War. In 1861 after the war had started, Elizabeth Cady Stanton acquiesced to the request from abolitionists led by Wendell Phillips to suspend agitation for women's rights and spend their energy focused on the war effort and the abolition of slavery. A practical thinker, she saw this move as a way to develop support from the abolitionist camp for the drive for suffrage once the war was over. She supported the war, calling it "music to my ears" as she looked forward to the powerful post-war coalition of abolitionists and women's rights activists. She later admitted to a critical Susan B. Anthony that her strategy of supporting the war in the hope of future gains for women was "a blunder."[46]

During the post-war period from 1865 to 1870, support from the abolitionists as a group did not materialize. Cady Stanton was more than discouraged; she was angry. Following an 1867 speech on women's rights, she was challenged by a man who declared that child-rearing was a more noble task for woman than was voting. He added that his wife had presented him with eight children. She looked him over and quipped, "I have met few men in my life worth repeating eight times."[47]

As the Reconstruction period progressed, Cady Stanton, as the emerging national leader of the women's rights movement, realized that the forces stacked against her were formidable. Betrayed by conservative women, Republican leaders, former abolitionists, freed slaves and Congressmen, her reactionary anger erupted. She helped to establish four organizations, worked for suffrage in Kansas, New York, and Washington, D.C., ran for Congress, edited The Revolution, worked for the passage of a sixteenth amendment for woman suffrage, and became more independent and accusative. As support for woman suffrage evaporated, she became a persistent, lone siren. Her logic, stated in a January 23, 1867 address to the New York State Legislature, was that

> "Women and negroes, being seven-twelfths of the people, are a majority; and according to our republican theory, are the rightful rulers of the nation."

Right—if they could vote. And therein laid her problem.[48] Powerful abolitionists and an ascending Republican Party supported black male suffrage, but not votes for women.

Cady Stanton raged,

> "The leading journals [praised] the patience and prudence, the executive ability, the loyalty and patriotism of the women of the League [who aided abolition], and yet these were the same women who, when demanding civil and political rights, privileges and immunities for themselves, had been uniformly denounced as 'unwise,' 'imprudent,' 'fanatical,' and 'impracticable'...."

In 1867, her efforts to lobby for woman suffrage in New York, and for both woman and black suffrage in Kansas, were defeated by white male legislators. Her reaction was to turn to the Democratic Party and George Francis Train for support. The New York Herald editorialized that the conservative Democrats could defeat the liberal Republicans

> "if only bold enough to take strong ground upon [woman suffrage] in favor of at least the same political rights to white women that Congress has given to Southern niggers."

The comment showed the power the issue had over the politics of the era.[49] Only a few of the abolitionists remained loyal to woman suffrage. Robert Purvis, Parker Pillsbury, and Samuel J. May were conspicuous in their supportive efforts, and were called by Purvis' biographer "moral heroes of the nineteenth century." By refusing to support woman suffrage, other giants like William Lloyd Garrison, Frederick Douglass, Wendell Phillips, and Gerrit Smith contradicted their moral principle of universal equality that recognized the justice of equal human rights.

Pillsbury argued, "It is no less an outrage now to rob woman of her just rights, than it was forty years ago to plunder the slave of his."[50]

The position of Cady Stanton's cousin Gerrit particularly irritated her because she thought she could trust in his support. On paper, his words and donations looked good; financial records indicate that he donated regularly in the late 1860s to the women's rights movement, and his previous writings showed the same. But, as previously indicated, he defected from support of women to support of black males for suffrage. Perhaps in opposition to his vacillation, his wife Ann sent to Congress in February of 1866 a petition favoring woman suffrage signed by twenty-eight women.[51]

In fairness to Smith, we must recognize that this defection was temporary; but that does not detract from the fact that he reneged on basic moral principles at a time when his quality of support was sorely needed.

It is possible to explain his actions, and, by inference, the actions of other abolitionists at that time. First, Smith was able to identify closely with black males. At times, he considered himself to be "colored." This produced a deep empathy. He realized that without the vote, they would not be able to defend themselves against the continuing prejudice against them after emancipation. Why did not this reasoning apply also to black women? Because, secondly, he could not identify himself as a woman—

black or white. And, third, his typically practical thought placed high value on his analysis of the available political support for the extension of suffrage. That is, public prejudice against suffrage for women was so intense that bundling black male and woman suffrage together would only ensure the defeat of both. So the salient question is, did this compromise of principle with practicality justify his opposition to woman suffrage? Cady Stanton didn't think so. Why not, she asked, remain true to principle and at least *try* to get women into the suffrage mix?

This illustrates the conflicted state of mind faced by many male abolitionists. The confrontation between practicality and principle produced what psychologists call an "approach-approach conflict." One desires two goals, but cannot have both. And without any precedent for successful social movement procedures, they stumbled around looking for solutions, angering some colleagues—or cousins—in the process. At the time, their latent support for issues of women's rights did not translate into action, much as in previous times some people's antislavery attitude may not have translated into abolition work because of their prejudice against blacks.

Thomas Wentworth Higginson was a Boston abolitionist and, along with Smith, a member of the Secret Six who had backed the raid on Harpers Ferry. He blamed women for the failure of suffrage, claiming "it is their unwillingness to ask for their rights which chiefly renders our legislators unwilling to concede them."

Does one need to *ask* for "their rights?" Do legislators hold the power to "concede" them? Those who believe in the universality of natural rights would answer no on both counts. The only proper role of government is to *protect* those rights. Hence, one can see the tyrannical role that white males assumed over women. In order to emphasize the inappropriateness of male power, the radical women activists revived the old revolutionary theme of taxation without representation. As Cady Stanton, Gage and Anthony put it,

> "surely the women of this republic, by their self-sacrifice and patriotism… have rightly earned a voice in the laws they [are] compelled to obey, and the Government they are taxed to support…."

Cady Stanton even went so far as to say that because women could not vote, they should not pay taxes. "Shall we," she asked, "purchase for ourselves a false power… by declaring in action that taxation without representation is just?"[52]

Because the national government in the post-war era was dominated by Republicans who had avoided supporting woman suffrage, Cady Stanton led an effort to convince the states to pass such legislation. Although the Constitution contained no statement that would prevent women from voting, she realized that efforts to argue at the Constitutional level would probably be wasted. She was proved right when a joint Congressional Judiciary Committee eventually issued a report on January 30, 1871 declaring that women were not United States citizens, but only "members of the state." This left decisions on suffrage up to each state.[53]

As a shining example of what could be, the 1776 New Jersey Constitution enfranchised "All inhabitants of this Colony of full age, who are worth fifty pounds…." It was the only place in the country where women were enfranchised in all elections before Wyoming was admitted as a state in 1890. In her Jan. 23, 1867 address to the New York State Legislature, Cady Stanton milked the point for all it was worth, saying,

> "Women and negroes exercised the right of suffrage in that state [for] thirty-one years—from 1776 to 1807….

Did the men of that period become mere satellites of
the dinner-pot, the wash-tub, or the spinning-wheel?
Were they dwarfed and crippled in body and soul,
while their enfranchised wives and mothers became giants in stature and intellect?... Were the laws of nature
suspended? Did the sexes change places? NO... And
the fact that women did vote there, created so slight
a ripple on the popular wave, and made so ordinary a
page in history, that probably nine-tenths of the people
of this country never heard of its existence...."[54]

At the time of her speech, New York State was planning a
state constitutional convention that would eventually refuse
to even consider the issue of woman suffrage. The state took a
mini-step in 1880 when the governor signed a bill to enfranchise
women in school board elections. In 1899, when a bill for tax-
payer suffrage was introduced in the New York State Senate, Gerrit Smith's daughter Elizabeth Smith Miller and granddaughter
Ann F. Miller testified there in favor of it, but it failed to pass.
New York State finally passed woman suffrage legislation in 1917,
fifteen years after Cady Stanton's death.[55]

The "Kansas campaign," as Cady Stanton called it, was
her biggest effort to push for the state-level enfranchisement of
women. In 1867, the Kansas legislature passed a Constitutional
amendment to remove the words "male" and "white" from voting restrictions, and submitted it to voters for ratification. If it
were ratified, both blacks and women would be enfranchised.
Cady Stanton and Susan B. Anthony spent two months traveling and lecturing in Kansas under frontier conditions in an
attempt to rally voters. Their living conditions were terrible.
Cady Stanton wrote to Elizabeth Smith Miller, "Oh,... the dirt,
the food!!"

The Republican Party dominated Kansas politics at the time, and was apathetic toward woman suffrage. Although Cady Stanton and Anthony tried to rally the support of liberal newspapers and Republican politicians, "they all preserved a stolid silence, and the Liberals of the State were… paralyzed by their example." When the referendum was defeated, neither the abolitionists nor the journalists offered any consoling words for women's loss, but the women who spoke during the campaign were reproached for having "killed negro suffrage."[56]

Cady Stanton now knew that expending energy working against conservative forces even at the state level was futile. One bright spot appeared in 1869 in the more liberal frontier territory of Wyoming. Legislation was passed there specifying "That every woman of the age of twenty-one years, residing in the territory, may at every election… cast her vote…." The editors of the "History of Woman Suffrage" reported that "woman has been recognized as a sovereign in her own right—an independent, responsible being—endowed with the capacity for self-government."

Two decades later, the state of Wyoming would be admitted to the Union as the first state to embrace woman suffrage, followed by Colorado in 1893, Utah in 1895, and Idaho in 1896. The obvious lesson was that where the popular culture was liberal enough, woman suffrage succeeded.[57]

To pursue this theme, Cady Stanton and Anthony formed the National Woman Suffrage Association in May of 1869. Centered in New York City, it sought a culture-wide revolution regarding prejudice against women. Because of Cady Stanton's radical stands and attitude about "tyrannical" men, the more conservative women's rights people led by Lucy Stone and Abby Kelley in Boston formed a rival group—the American Woman Suffrage Association. Its main goal was woman suffrage. But whereas the

AWSA worked mainly at the state level, the NWSA lobbied for a federal amendment.[58]

Cady Stanton also attempted to build an alliance with the emerging labor movement in 1868, assuming that human rights issues could create coalitions among oppressed groups. But the mainly white male National Labor Union rejected woman suffrage as one of their goals.

Elizabeth's last effort at organizational activity occurred in 1890, when AWSA and NWSA merged to form the National American Woman Suffrage Association. The idea was largely that of Susan B. Anthony, and the goal was to create a large and cooperative resource base for the pursuit of suffrage. Cady Stanton was not enthusiastic about the merger due to her age and her interest in a broader spectrum of goals than just the vote. She did allow herself to be its figurehead president, but she did not become involved in its work. "I have outgrown the suffrage association," she said, "and no longer belong in its fold with its limitations." In looking back on it, Cady Stanton saw the post-war period of women's rights activity as one of hard work and continuous discouragement.[59]

On March 15, 1869, Indiana Congressional Representative George W. Julian submitted to Congress a joint Senate/House resolution to enfranchise women. As "Article 16," it was to become the sixteenth amendment to the United States Constitution:

> "The Right of Suffrage in the United States shall
> be based on citizenship, and shall be regulated by
> Congress; and all citizens of the United States, whether
> native or naturalized, shall enjoy this right equally
> without any distinction or discrimination whatever
> founded on sex."[60]

Little action had been taken on this measure three years later in 1872, when Matilda Joslyn Gage wrote to the Secretary of the

Republican National Committee to offer the National Woman Suffrage Association's aid in a public campaign to secure support for woman suffrage. Even though the Republicans were the "liberals" of that time, they succeeded in ignoring such pleas for the next two decades. The proposed amendment languished in committee until 1887, when the Senate defeated it by a vote of sixteen in favor, twenty-four opposed, and twenty-six abstentions! We wonder whether the vote reflected cowardice or conflicted minds. It certainly sanctioned the continuing bias against women held by white males in positions of power.[61]

Cady Stanton had faced this bias at many points during the Reconstruction era. It was similar to the bias that prevented free blacks from exercising their rights of citizenship—and from the same source.

At the Independence Hall celebration of the national centennial in Philadelphia in 1876, she had drafted a declaration of women's rights that focused on the continued denial of suffrage. It was ignored.

In a letter to Anthony in late 1880, she felt pessimistic about the chances for suffrage in the United States because both the Democratic and Republican parties were too conservative to enfranchise women.

On a trip to England in 1882, she noted that male leaders of government and business institutions there were opposed to woman suffrage.

In 1885, Cady Stanton and other leaders of the women's rights movement had two hearings before the Committee on Grievances of the New York State legislature in Albany. Cady Stanton recalled that they were told, in effect,

> "'Be patient, dear sisters,… this is simply a question of time. What may not come in your day, future generations will surely possess.' It is always pleasant to know

that our descendants are to enjoy life, liberty, and happiness; but, when one is grasping for one breath of freedom, this reflection is not satisfying."

Her discouragement seemed unending. And to illustrate the gulf in thought that separated the perspectives of males from females during this era, when Cady Stanton was asked by Senator Zebulon Vance at a Congressional committee meeting in Washington, D.C. on February 8, 1890, "Would women be willing to go to war if they had the ballot?," she replied, "We would decide first whether there should be war."[62]

The continuing male bias against women endangered suffrage on many fronts during reconstruction. In 1876, the National Woman Suffrage Association "Resolved, That the women of this nation, in 1876, have greater cause for discontent, rebellion and revolution, than the men of 1776." One reason for this came from what women called their "New Departure" approach to suffrage in 1871. This claim was that the Fourteenth Amendment granted woman suffrage because it protected rights of citizenship without any reference to sex. This logic made sense until 1875 when the United States Supreme Court, in the case of Minor v. Happersett, ruled that suffrage was not among the rights of citizenship. The members of the Supreme Court were, of course, all male.

This was a curious decision when one considers that the Federal Amnesty Act of 1872 had re-enfranchised nearly five thousand former Confederate male leaders. As Wagner put it, "If Congress could refranchise traitors, could it not franchise loyal women?"

Between 1870 and 1890, woman suffrage amendments were defeated by public referendum in eight states. Cady Stanton summed it up by saying, "It is very humiliating for women… to have their sacred rights at the mercy of a masculine oligarchy."[63]

Perhaps the most poignant discouragement of the era resulted from the effort made by some suffrage leaders to go to the polls and vote. During the antislavery movement, women had learned that civil disobedience against unjust laws was an effective technique of resistance and protest. In 1871, the National Woman Suffrage Association was urging women to vote, thereby agitating for change and forcing men to show just cause for preventing citizens from voting. Many women activists voted in elections in 1872, including Sojourner Truth, Sarah and Angelina Grimké, and Susan B. Anthony. Because of her high profile in the women's rights movement, Anthony became a test case in court for woman suffrage.[64]

On November 5, 1872, Susan B. Anthony and six other women voted in the presidential election in Rochester, New York. Anthony proudly wrote to Cady Stanton that she "had gone and done it!!" On November 28, all seven women were arrested by Federal Marshal Elisha Keeney on $500 bail, to appear in United States District Court on January 21, 1873. Anthony's trial of prosecution started on June 18, 1873 in Canandaigua on the charge of having "knowingly, wrongfully, and unlawfully" voted.

The judge was Ward Hunt, referred to by Cady Stanton as "a small-brained, pale faced… man." This was his first criminal case, and he issued the decision of guilty without consulting the jury. "[W]ith remarkable forethought," said Cady Stanton, "he had penned his decision before hearing it."[65]

Anthony was fined $100 plus court costs, to which she immediately responded, "I shall never pay a dollar of your unjust penalty." Although Hunt tried to silence her, she said:

> "Yes, your honor, I have many things to say; for in
> your ordered verdict of guilty, you have trampled
> under foot every vital principle of our government.
> My natural rights, my civil rights, my political rights,

my judicial rights, are all alike ignored. Robbed of the
fundamental privilege of citizenship, I am degraded
from the status of a citizen to that of a subject; and not
only myself individually, but all of my sex, are, by your
honor's verdict, doomed to political subjection under
this, so-called, form of government."[66]

In a gesture of support, Gerrit Smith sent to Anthony money
to cover her costs. He knew of her intent not to pay, and instruct-
ed her to use the gift as she saw fit. On March 2, 1874, President
Grant directed the Attorney General to forgive Anthony's fine,
thereby pardoning her of the crime of having voted.[67]

Smith's gift of money to Anthony is curious, for he knew of
her refusal to pay the fine. Most likely, it was a palliative move
for his own conscience for having opposed woman suffrage at its
most critical time. It served the function of a 'pill' to lessen the
severity of his self-inflicted pain without curing anything.

It was after the ratification of the Fifteenth Amendment on
March 30, 1870 enfranchising black males that Smith softened
his opposition to woman suffrage and began to apologize to
them. In November of 1872, he told Lucy Stone that he was too
old to be able to travel to St. Louis to attend a woman's rights
convention, and gave her a figurative "pat on the back"—really
a gesture of dominance—saying, "Let woman be of good cheer.
She will not have to wait for the ballot much longer." He probably
realized that it was too late for him to do anything meaningful
about it anyway. He had been suffering attacks of vertigo, and
would die of a stroke in late 1874. But his optimism about a better, more equitable future remained. His "innocent hope" assured
him that "Dramshops... would soon be overthrown..., [and that]
equal rights will soon be accorded to the black man everywhere.
Best of all, the ballot [will belong to women]."[68]

Words were cheap, so he tried to cheer up those he had so deeply disappointed not long ago. Smith had a keen legal mind, so he spent much time and ink on the logic of why women should be enfranchised. One wonders what happened to the relevance of all these arguments between 1865 and 1870.

Voting, Smith said, is not, as men claim, "an inferior right" that women should not be concerned about. "The chief use of suffrage is in the selection of rules…. The disenfranchised lie… at the mercy of those who have usurped the <u>exclusive</u> franchise." One reason that only men can vote, he told Susan B. Anthony, was because their "superior physical strength" allows them to be dominant. A second reason was that "Constitutions, being man-made, are made almost universally, in the interest of defeating and ignoring this claim [for suffrage] on the part of woman."

Then he admitted "that such things go somewhat toward making me ashamed of being a man." He must have thought that confessions of the power-hungry motives of males would absolve him of guilt for having defected from the cause of women.[69]

Whatever the reasons, he went on in letters to Anthony about the connections between constitutions, natural law, and human rights as he attempted to assure her that her act of voting was legitimate. The argument against woman suffrage made by most men was simply that the Constitution prevented it. But the Constitution, Smith claimed, "is not the end of the law…." There exists no legal appeal for natural rights. "The appeal from the statute is to the constitution; the appeal from the constitution is to the law of our being and to Him who is the source of all law."

Interestingly, even as his focus was on women, he still could not get the power of a male deity out of his mind.

Smith continued,

> "As they are… infinitely above and infinitely anterior
> to all constitutions, [natural rights] can neither be

made nor unmade, created or destroyed, by constitutions…. All admit that a statute is not conclusive, and that what in it violates the constitution is to be rejected. So also should all admit that the constitution is not conclusive and that what in it violates natural law or natural rights should likewise be rejected."

Smith agreed with Anthony and Cady Stanton that women who preferred not to be enfranchised perpetuated their "degradation and required submission." He viewed them as "perverted and befooled by their <u>ladyism</u>," and in need of "more sympathy with the toiling masses of women; and less aristocratic self-idolatry."[70]

All of this verbiage from Gerrit Smith sounded good as a justification of Anthony's act of voting, and a rationalization of his—and others'—critically timed pause in their support of woman suffrage. Perhaps he realized that the effect of that pause by such influential opinion leaders as himself, Frederick Douglass, and Wendell Phillips would retard the acquisition of woman suffrage for over five decades. But his concern and apologies came too late. He was too old to carry the ball of reform much further, and anti-woman bias in public opinion had been reinforced once more.

The last two decades of Elizabeth Cady Stanton's life were relatively quiet compared to her frantic pace between 1840 and 1880. She did much writing, publishing the two-volume "Woman's Bible" in 1895, and her autobiography "Eighty Years and More" in 1898. Her health failing in late 1902, she wrote to President Theodore Roosevelt asking him to use part of his next address to Congress to endorse the woman suffrage amendment to the United States Constitution. She died on October 26, 1902.[71]

Although she was gone, Cady Stanton's younger colleagues

carried on the fight for woman suffrage. Elizabeth Smith Miller attended several women's rights conventions and hosted gatherings of women activists at her lakeside estate in Geneva, New York before her death in 1911. Her daughter Ann Fitzhugh Miller spoke before the United States Senate Committee on Woman Suffrage in February of 1906 regarding the submission of a woman suffrage amendment to the Constitution. The Nineteenth Amendment was finally submitted by Congress to state legislatures for ratification on June 4, 1919. It read:

"The right of citizens of the United States to vote shall not be denied or abridged by the United States or by any State on account of sex."

Secretary of State Bainbridge Colby announced ratification on August 26, 1920.[72]

With ratification of the Nineteenth Amendment within reach, the call for the "Victory Convention" of the National American Woman Suffrage Association was issued for February 12-18, 1920 in Chicago:

> "Suffragists, hear this call to a suffrage convention! The officers of the National American Woman Suffrage Association hereby call the State auxiliaries, through their elected delegates, to meet in annual convention at Chicago, Congress Hotel, February 12th to 18th, inclusive. In other days our members and friends have been summoned to annual conventions to disseminate the propaganda for their common cause, to cheer and encourage each other, to strengthen their organized influence, to counsel as to ways and means of insuring further progress. At this time they are called to rejoice that the struggle is over, the aim achieved and the women of the nation about to enter into the enjoyment of their hard-earned political

liberty. Of all the conventions held within the past
fifty-one years, this will prove the most momentous.
Few people live to see the actual and final realization
of hopes to which they have devoted their lives. That
privilege is ours."[73]

The shame of the nation is that it was not Elizabeth Cady
Stanton's as well.

Epilogue

On this beautiful, warm, spring morning I sit in Gerrit's Smith's Land Office in Peterboro. The rising deep yellow sun shines through the east window's rippled glass panes, painting a portion of the antique brick floor in rosy hues. Built in 1804 by Gerrit's father, Peter with the aid of slave labor, this small, unpretentious brick building stands as a memorial to those giants of American history who dedicated their lives to the eternal battles to secure human rights and social justice.

I sit where Gerrit sat at his desk. Pictures of people who stood on these bricks with Gerrit stare at me from the wall, seeming to ask if their efforts to aid the oppressed resulted in any lasting change. John Brown wonders if Smith's support of his Harpers Ferry raid triggered any action to end slavery. Harriet Tubman nods in appreciation of the moral support of the Peterboro community for the former slaves she led to Canada. Frederick Douglass folds his arms in regal dignity and thanks Gerrit for helping to finance his radical journalism.

Lingering memories of these giants fill the room with awe. It is quiet here now, but as I listen through the silence, I can hear faint voices of people whose presence graced this room. Native Americans met here in council with Peter Smith, seeking justice for their people. Runaway slaves, terrified of almost everyone, bravely stood by this desk requesting help; the shouts of slave owners chasing their property echo from these walls. Women fighting for equality and the right to vote petitioned Smith for his aid. Poor people needing financial help for their families begged for Smith's assistance—which he usually provided.

The social movements discussed and pursued in this room included the abolition of slavery, the limitation of the use of alcohol, the founding of political parties, the benefits of open, integrated education, and the pursuit of equal rights for all people—especially women. In that vein, we must meet another frequent visitor to this office.

The year was 1839. An attractive twenty-three year old woman with a keen and developing interest in human rights sat here with Gerrit, telling him how she appreciated the opportunity to meet and discuss issues with his abolitionist friends. Touching Elizabeth Cady's arm, Gerrit asked her to come with him to the third floor of his nearby residence to meet someone special.

Elizabeth was about to have an encounter that would shape her entire life. Harriet Powell, an escaped slave, was waiting in the house while Gerrit's staff prepared transportation for her to Canada. Elizabeth talked with Harriet for hours, learning of her abuses as a slave—and as a woman—under the power of white males. Elizabeth soon became dedicated to the emancipation of both slaves and women from a world of injustice.

Today, this tiny land office in Peterboro, New York memorializes these two cousins of reform—two of the most radical thinkers and actors in the two most important social movements in the history of the United States. Women and African Americans especially, and all of us generally, owe a debt of gratitude to Gerrit and Elizabeth that can probably never be paid. But that would not bother the crusading reformers, who focused so intensely on the goals of abolition and women's rights that those around them who could not—or would not—see the big picture of human oppression called them "crazy." They donated their own resources of money, time, oratory, and composition to causes they could not resist—and for people they did not know.

During his lifetime, Gerrit Smith gave away nearly one billion dollars (in today's value) to people who were in some way oppressed. Cady Stanton gave an equal measure of her skills in social agitation and journalism. They both fought prejudice and discrimination wherever they saw it.

William Lloyd Garrison called Cady Stanton "a fearless woman [who] goes for woman's rights with all her soul."

She once asked, "if there is no justice in heaven or on earth that this [discrimination] should be permitted through the centuries."

Susan B. Anthony referred to her as "the acknowledged leader of progressive thought and demand in regard to all matters pertaining to the absolute freedom of women."[1]

Both Smith and Cady Stanton were practical, progressive thinkers who channeled their actions through political activity to achieve reforms. Their vision of a more just and equitable society made them demand more than people in power were willing to allow or concede. And therein lies the essence of reform as opposed to revolution: They used established institutions to pursue reasonable goals toward "liberty and justice for all."

Whereas Cady Stanton and Smith were giants in the field of social reform and deserve deep respect for their sacrifices and accomplishments, we need to be careful not to cast their images as 'perfect saints'. In doing so, we would lose sight of their humanity—and diminish their value for us as role models.

The quality of thought that united these cousins in reform activity was empathy. If we could all emulate them, life would be more peaceful everywhere. But even for them, empathy sometimes failed; they both exhibited difficulty in controlling tendencies toward racism and sexism.

Prejudice against others who are not like ourselves is universal. Every human era has had its wars of religion, politics, or economic systems based in differences in culture. It is the epitome of human failure that we all come from the same seed, but cannot get along.

Gerrit Smith noted in his "Religion of Reason" that if diversity among constituents produced stability in natural ecosystems, it seemed that we could manage the same dynamic in human social systems. Yet we cannot even recognize natural equality among diverse parts of our own culture, and must resort to legislation in the attempt to achieve it. Our great deficiency is that we cannot succeed at seeing ourselves in others, or others in ourselves.

As intensely committed to the implementation of human rights as Smith and Cady Stanton were, they were still shackled by limitations on empathy. Both at times showed evidence of racism and sexism. Cady Stanton labeled all men as "tyrants," and black males as "Sambo." Smith had difficulty holding women consistently on an equal plane with black males. It seems strange in the twenty-first century that so many avid advocates of human rights during the nineteenth century could be intensely concerned about racism, yet not include sexism in their thoughts—or vice versa. But we must remember that anti-women or anti-black feelings were considered normal then. Both blacks and women were pitied by white males for having been born without sufficient natural abilities for survival.

Our inability to *feel* one another's perspectives, combined with the belief that all people deserve equity, leads to the need for reform as perceived by the Smiths and Cady Stantons of the nineteenth century. As Cady Stanton eloquently wrote,

> "It was not from ignorance of the unequal laws... that
> our best men stood silent in [the suffrage] campaign;...
> it was not from lack of money and power, of eloquence

of pen and tongue, nor of an intellectual conviction
that our cause was just, that they came not to the
rescue, but because in their heart of hearts they did not
grasp the imperative necessity of woman's demand for
that protection which the ballot alone can give; they
did not feel for <u>her</u> the degradation of disfranchisement."

So it was then, because most men could not conceive of
themselves as women, a point that still seems to characterize our
society today.[2]

A good question is: How are we doing today with the human rights goals sought by Smith and Cady Stanton over a century and a half ago? According to twentieth century feminist
Gloria Steinem, there is still a "conservative war on women"
that requires "a change of consciousness" if we are to succeed
at implementing equal rights. The problem, she claims, is still
a matter of identity.

> "We've learned that women can do what men can do,
> but we haven't convinced most of the country that men
> can do what women can do…. Sometimes a Mom will
> come up to me and say her teenage daughter doesn't
> know who I am. I don't care if she doesn't know who I
> am. I care if she knows who she is."

Discrimination against contemporary women, Steinem says,
is "not different in kind" from previous historical eras. "It's a matter of degree."[3]

A recent study by the National Women's Law Center documents the fact that health insurance companies can deny applications on the grounds that the applicant is a woman. At the time
of this first edition, thirty-seven states allow health insurance

companies to refuse coverage for women, or charge them more than men for identical coverage.

Reasons for this inequitable treatment include the fact that women receive more injuries than men from domestic abuse, "pre-existing conditions" are more frequent in women, women take more medications than men, and women seek the aid of doctors more frequently than men. Such treatment of women is certainly insensitive to issues of equality.[4]

Insensitivity toward women also appears regarding issues of birth control and abortion. "Reproductive freedom," said Steinem, "is a fundamental human right…. But there is a backlash against it from patriarchical religions that have enshrined the idea of a male God and control over women." At a February 12, 2012 House of Representatives hearing on birth control, the panel of presenters consisted of five males. Is not the woman's perspective important?

And on an old theme that reveals discrimination, ninety-four percent of injuries sustained due to domestic violence are incurred by women. Three women die every day in the United States as a result of domestic violence, and one in four will experience it at some time during her life. In February of 2012, all Republican Party members on the United States Senate Judiciary Committee refused to support reauthorization of the 1994 Violence Against Women Act because of its extension of protective services to gay and transgendered persons.

And in regard to racism, it is probable that nearly every black adult in the United States today can relate incidents of discrimination against them.[5]

Elizabeth Cady Stanton and Gerrit Smith would be disappointed if not appalled by these facts, and would know where to start working if they could. From Smith's lofty economic vantage point he could see many categories of people who needed help toward achieving equitable social treatment. With characteristic optimism, he committed his pen, his time, and his money to their causes. Cady Stanton's strongest personal trait was self-confidence, and as an agitator, her forte was controversy. She outraged social conservatives and sometimes even her liberal colleagues with her radical stands. Her ethic of self-sovereignty pervaded her speeches and writings, and defeat only intensified her resolve.

What Cady Stanton and Smith saw as a potential solution to issues of equitable social treatment of all people, they could not achieve. They both dreamed of a grand coalition of all oppressed groups of people into a powerful and unbeatable political force. Cady Stanton tried to focus on a wide variety of women's rights issues instead of just suffrage, and even had thoughts of uniting various pressure groups. Believing all reforms were linked, she wrote to Susan B. Anthony, "the period for all these fragmentary reforms is ended. Agitation of the broader question… is now in order…. It is impossible to have equal rights for all under our present competitive system." Smith saw a powerful unity in diversity, as he indicated in his Religion of Reason. If oppressed groups could come together, he thought, a new oneness of purpose could aid success.[6]

Although the 'rainbow coalition' to end white male supremacy dreamed of by our nineteenth-century cousins never did come about, there are some tentative signs in the early twenty-first century that opposition to such supremacy is waning. Interracial marriages in the United States have increased from 3% of all marriages in 1980, to 16.5 percent in 2010, suggesting that "Guess Who's Coming to Dinner" might not be as threatening a question as it was when Stanley Kramer directed the movie in 1967.[7]

In October of 2011, Abby Kelley Foster was inducted into the National Abolition Hall of Fame and Museum in Peterboro,

New York, and into the Women's Hall of Fame in Seneca Falls, New York. These were separate decisions that reflect her significance in two historical realms. And in the political coup of two and a half centuries, the United States now has its first African American President. The election of Barack Obama in 2008 has disrupted centuries of white male supremacy, and challenged any claims of the supposed disabilities of any minority group.

A major opponent to the pursuit of equal rights for oppressed minorities has been—and still is—the Christian Church. As Cady Stanton pointed out so clearly, the Bible supports the subservience of women, the dominance of men, and generally pictures both God and Jesus Christ as white males. And one group today that faces intense discrimination from Christianity is the gay/lesbian/transgendered minority. It is reasonable to question whether there will ever be a coalition of forces favoring equal rights for all oppressed minorities that would include the Christian Church.

One feature of social life in the United States that seems apparent to this author is that during the nineteenth century, discrimination against women was more intense than discrimination against black people. And it may still be. Any daily newspaper or news report would give clues to Gerrit Smith and Elizabeth Cady Stanton concerning what they should write about.

Their friend and colleague in reform Lydia Maria Child noted that a liberal, human rights candidate was nominated for President of the United States in 1856. Then she added, "For the sake of… freedom in peril… let's vote!" She knew, of course, that she could not, and vowed to return in the afterlife and "rap at the ballot box."[8]

I suspect that if Lydia Maria Child or Elizabeth Cady Stanton or Gerrit Smith were around today, they would still be rapping.

NOTES

Abbreviations used in Notes

HWS, History of Woman Suffrage
SU, Syracuse University, Department of Special Collections
MCHS, Madison County Historical Society
ECS, Elizabeth Cady Stanton
GS, Gerrit Smith
ACS, Ann Carroll Smith
ESM, Elizabeth Smith Miller
SLC, Speeches, Letters, and Circulars. Copy in possession of the
  author, and at the Peterboro Historical Society.
SBA, Susan B. Anthony
WLG, William Lloyd Garrison

Preface

1. The editors of volume I are Elizabeth Cady Stanton, Susan B. Anthony and Matilda Joslyn Gage.

2. See the three books by Dann listed in the bibliography.

3. See the Elizabeth Griffith biography of Elizabeth Cady Stanton, and the Norman K. Dann biography of Gerrit Smith listed in the bibliography.

Chapter 1

1. ECS to John Greenleaf Whittlier, July 11, 1840 in Griffith, 7.

2. Banner, 10; Griffith, 4, 7.

3. Griffith, 8-9; Ulrich, 139-140; Kern, 22; Stanton, Eighty Years..., 14, 21-24; Banner, 14.

4. Griffith, 17-21; Banner, 12-14; Stanton, Eighty Years..., 43-44.

5. Banner, 7; Griffith, 7, 17-19; Stanton, Eighty Years..., 18.

6. Colman, 59; Griffith, 73; HWS, I, 459; Stanton, Eighty Years..., 145.

7. Griffith, 116.

8. HWS, I, 421-422.

9. Wellman, 42-43; Griffith, 26.

10. ECS to ACS, March 4, 1840 in Wellman, 44; Stanton, Eighty Years..., 55.

11. Griffith, 33; H.B. Stanton to GS, April 17, 1840; May 10, 1840, SU.

12. Wellman, 220.

13. Griffith, 165; Banner, 121; ECS to GS, Jan. 25, 1879, SU; ECS to Amy Post, June 1, 1860 in Griffith, 99; Stanton, Eighty Years..., 282.

14. Griffith, 163.

15. Faulkner, 160.

16. ECS to Wendell Phillips, Aug. 10, 1860 in Gordon, 437; Griffith, xx; ECS to GS, Dec. 16, 1861, SU.

17. ECS to Mary Ann White Johnson and the Ohio Women's Convention, April 7, 1850 in Gordon, 165; ECS, "Address to the Legislature on Women's Right of Suffrage," February 18, 1860 in DuBois and Smith, eds., 172.

18. Stanton, Eighty Years…, 287, 288, 295; HWS, II.

19. New York Times, Oct. 27, 1902.

20. I have written extensively on Gerrit Smith's life in Practical Dreamer. The material covered here is well documented therein.

Chapter 2

1. Stanton, Eighty Years…, 344 (this brook still "creeps slowly" through the front yard of the Cottage Across the Brook, which is the home of the author and his wife Dorothy H. Willsey-Dann.); Banner, 1, 16.

2. Stanton, Eighty Years…, 51, 48, 49, 58, 48.

3. Stanton, HWS, I, 471n; Frothingham, 142.

4. Stanton, Eighty Years…, 50-51.

5. Stanton, Eighty Years…, 344; ECS to Peter Smith, Jan. 27, 1836, SU.

6. Stanton, Eighty Years…, 54, 56-57.

7. ECS to ACS, March 4, 1840, SU.

8. Griffith, 107, 183, 206; Eighty Years…, 317.

9. Robertson, 53.

10. Davis, 222.

11. HWS, I, 472.

12. Stanton, HWS, IV, 203; ECS to ESM + C.D. Miller, Feb. 3, 1845 in Gordon, 50, 51; ECS to ACS, Sept. 20, no year, SU.

13. Stanton, Eighty Years…, 255; HWS, IV, 227.

Chapter 3

1. Stanton, <u>Eighty Years</u>…, 340-341.

2. For instance, the alliance between John Brown and blacks, Gerrit Smith and Frederick Douglass, and the connections within the underground railroad process.

3. Wyatt-Brown, ix, 62-63, x.

4. Griffith, 141.

5. Stanton, <u>The Woman's Bible</u>, 287; Griffith, 162.

6. Newman, 108.

7. Stanton, <u>HWS</u>, IV, xxii; Stanton, <u>Eighty Years</u>…, 208.

8. Stanton, <u>Eighty Years</u>…, 306.

9. Stanton, <u>Eighty Years</u>…, 196.

10. ECS to GS, Dec. 21, 1855, SU.

11. Stanton, address to the American Anti-Slavery Society, May 8, 1860; Stanton, <u>Eighty Years</u>…, 204.

Chapter 4

1. Ulrich, xiii, xxi.

2. Macionis, 318-319.

3. Ecker.

4. Kitch, 70; Ulrich, 157.

5. <u>The Liberator</u>, Sept. 6, 1834.

6. ECS to Mary Ann White Johnson and the Ohio Women's Convention, April 7, 1850, in Gordon, 164.

7. Wellman, 137; Stanton, <u>Eighty Years</u>…, 25.

8. Wyatt-Brown, 66; advertisements in possession of the author, 1870s.

9. Abzug, <u>Cosmos</u>…, 187; Griffith, 15, xiv; Faulkner, 8; Davis, 153; Lemons, 45; ECS to GS, Dec. 21, 1855, SU.

10. Stanton, "Perhaps," 1848, in Gordon, 99; Davis, 120.

11. Stanton, "Address to AERA," May 12, 1869, in DuBois and Smith, eds., 193.

12. ECS to SBA, Dec. 1, 1853, in DuBois, ed., 57; Eighty Years…, 207.

13. Dann, Practical…, 439; Abzug, Cosmos…, 210-213.

14. Abzug, Cosmos…, 217; Sarah Grimké to GS, in The Lily, Oct. 1, 1856.

15. Abzug, Cosmos…, 216.

16. Stanton, "Perhaps," 1848, in Gordon, 113; Stanton, "Address Delivered at Seneca Falls," July 19, 1848, in DuBois, ed., 28; Stanton, The Woman's Bible, in DuBois and Smith, eds., 294.

17. Stanton, "Ruth Hall," Feb. 1855, in Gordon, 297-298; Ulrich, 28; Griffith, 84; Colman, 80.

18. Stanton, "Ruth Hall," Feb. 1855, in Gordon, 299; Stanton, "The Other Side of the Woman Question," 1879, in DuBois and Smith, eds., 238.

19. Dann, Practical Dreamer; Stanton, "Perhaps," 1848, in Gordon, 111.

20. SBA to Aaron McLean, in Colman, 28-29; Stanton, The Woman's Bible, in DuBois and Smith, eds., 293-294; Stanton, "Our Girls," 1880, website 3; Abzug, Cosmos…, 183.

21. Stanton, "Legislative Doings," May, 1850, in Gordon; Stanton, speech at Woman's Suffrage Convention in Washington, D.C., 1868, website 2.

22. ECS to ESM, April 15, 1847, in Gordon, 62-63; ECS to SBA, Dec. 23, 1859, in DuBois, ed., 69.

23. Friedman, 130; Robertson, 47.

24. Banner, 58.

25. Friedman, 132-153.

26. Stanton, "To the Women of the State of New York," Frederick Douglass' Paper, Dec. 22, 1854; GS to ECS, Dec. 1, 1855; GS to SBA, May 7, 1853, SU.

27. Stanton, "Address to the New York Legislature," Feb. 14, 1854, in DuBois, ed., 50.
28. Ulrich, 33.
29. Wellman, 122.
30. Abzug, <u>Cosmos</u>..., 217; Colman, 22.
31. Davis, 94-98; Faulkner, 151; Sernett, 77.
32. Colman, 122-123.
33. Stanton, "Perhaps," 1848 in Gordon, 106; Stanton, "I Have All the Rights I Want," 1859 in Gordon, 405.
34. Colman, 134; Faulkner, 157.
35. Braude.
36. Coleman, 82-83; Griffith, 95.
37. Kitch, 181, 183, 186, 244, 251; Hodges, 8; Lemons, 40-41.

Chapter 5

1. Wellman, 157, 165, 168, 191-192; Griffith, 50-51; Stanton, <u>Eighty Years</u>..., 117, 118.
2. Wellman, 191.
3. Stanton, <u>Eighty Years</u>..., 118; Davis, 59; Smith, March 11, 1850, MCHS.
4. Banner, 45; Faulkner, 140.
5. Griffith, 58-60; Stanton, <u>Eighty Years</u>..., 118; Gordon, 88; <u>Oneida Whig</u>, Aug. 1, 1848; Wellman, 198, 207-210.
6. Griffith, 64-65.
7. <u>HWS</u>, I, 461.
8. <u>HWS</u>, IV, xiii.
9. DuBois, ed., 102; Stanton, <u>Eighty Years</u>..., 323.
10. ECS to the Woman's Rights Convention at Akron, OH, May 25, 1851 in <u>HWS</u>, I, 816.
11. Davis, 75; DuBois, ed., 79.
12. Davis, 108-109, 80.

13. H.B. Stanton to GS, Dec. 18, 1845, SU.
14. GS to WLG, Nov. 19, 1854 in <u>HWS</u>, I, 620, 526-527.
15. GS to ECS, Dec. 1, 1855, SU.
16. ECS to Martha Wright, March 21, 1871 in Griffith, 64.
17. GS to ECS, May 3, 1860, SU; GS to George G. Ritchie, April 15, 1847, SU; SBA to GS, July 1, 1863, SU; <u>HWS</u>, II, 357, 757, 923-924; <u>HWS</u>, I, 823-825.
18. Lucy Stone to Samuel May, Aug. 2, 1852, SU; SBA to GS, Sept. 5, 1856, SU.
19. GS to ECS, May 3, 1860, SU.
20. GS to ECS, Dec. 1, 1855, SU.
21. ECS to GS, Dec. 21, 1855, SU.
22. GS to ECS, Dec. 1, 1855, SU.
23. GS to county magistrates, May 1, 1849; Jan. 4, 1850, SU.
24. Abzug, <u>Passionate</u>…, 269; Davis, 61.
25. Allen, 213-214; Wagner, <u>Sisters</u>…, 57.
26. Wagner, <u>Sisters</u>…, 53-54; George-Kanentiio, 54-55.
27. George-Kanentiio, 68.
28. George-Kanentiio, 53-58, 96, 129.
29. Wagner, <u>Sisters</u>…, 46-47, 82; George-Kanentiio, 57.
30. George-Kanentiio, 100-104.
31. Wagner, <u>Sisters</u>…, 75, 89-92.
32. Matilda Joslyn Gage quoted in Wagner, <u>She Who</u>…, 34; George-Kanentiio, 64.
33. Abigail Adams to John Adams, march 31, 1776 in <u>HWS</u>, III, 19-20; Stanton, <u>Eighty Years</u>…, 330; Colman, 69.
34. Stanton, "Address of Women to the International Council of Women," March 25, 1880 in DuBois, ed., 210, 212.
35. Colman, 50, 71; <u>HWS</u>, I, 462.
36. Colman, 49; <u>HWS</u>, I, 75.
37. Faulkner, 149-151; Colman, 64; <u>HWS</u>, I, 820-821.
38. <u>HWS</u>, I, 517n, 852-854.

39. Griffith, 112; Banner, 93.

40. Baker, 122-123; Griffith, xiv; HWS, V, 1.

41. Griffith, 144.

42. Griffith, 198; Colman, 188-189.

43. HWS, I, 685; DuBois, ed., 46-47.

44. Stanton, Eighty Years…, 238-242.

45. HWS, I, 16, 63-64; Anthony, 2-6, 105-107; Wellman, 135-137.

46. Wagner, Matilda…, 10, 29; Colman, 149-150; DuBois, ed., 107.

47. Smith, "The Crime of the Abolitionists," Oct. 22, 1835, SU.

48. ECS to SBA, Dec. 28, 1869 in Colman, 129; Robertson, 145-147.

49. DuBois, ed., 109; HWS, I, 604; Wagner, Sisters…, 19-20.

50. Colman, 161-162; Davis, 181-182.

51. Davis, 178-181; DuBois, ed., 193.

Chapter 6

1. The Liberator, March 27, 1846.

2. Faulkner, 68, 216-217.

3. HWS, I, 52; Griffith, 86; Faulkner, 64-65.

4. Beck, 74-75; Faulkner, 72; Wellman, 52.

5. George Thompson to WLG, Oct. 22, 1835 in Letters…, 115-116; See Kate Clifford Larson, Bound for the Promised Land, New York: Ballantine Books, 2004; Nell Irvin Painter, Sojourner Truth: A Life, A Symbol, New York: W.W. Norton, 1996; web site 4.

6. Swerdlow, in Yellin and VanHorne, eds., 32n; HWS, I, 101.

7. Ulrich, 135-136.

8. Griffith, 41; Wellman, 50.

9. Faulkner, 4-5, 108, 115, 126, 130, 138, 215.

10. <u>HWS</u>, I, 38; Child, iv; Beck, 68-71, 75.

11. McFeely, 9.

12. Douglass, 391; Foner, P., 709; Douglass, 427.

13. <u>HWS</u>, I, 81, 102.

14. Gordon, 587; Stanton, <u>Eighty Years</u>…, 72.

15. ECS to GS, Aug. 3, 1840, SU; Robertson, 32.

16. Banner, 69; ECS to Mary Ann White Johnson and the Ohio Woman's Convention, April 7, 1850 in Gordon, 165.

17. ECS address to the American Anti-Slavery Society, May 18, 1860; Griffith, 44.

18. ECS to Elizabeth Pease, Feb. 12, 1842 in Wellman, 159, and DuBois, ed., 10.

19. Stanton, <u>Eighty Years</u>…, 70-71, 146.

20. Wellman, 55-56; Beck, 66; Friedman, 158-159; Davis, 42-43.

21. Faulkner, 66-67, 78; Wellman, 48.

22. Sterling, 83-84.

23. Davis, 121-122; Faulkner, 181.

24. Hewitt in Yellin and VanHorne, eds., 26, 29; Lemons, 19.

25. Faulkner, 169.

26. <u>The Liberator</u>, March 1, 1850; Faulkner, 98; ECS to ES(M), May 28, 1842 in Gordon.

27. Stanton, <u>Eighty Years</u>…, 186.

28. Friedman, 137.

29. Petrulinois, 387.

30. Hansen in Yellin and VanHorne, eds., 54.

31. Mayer, 282; Friedman, 157; Stanton, "Address to the Eighth National Woman's Rights Convention," May 13, 1858 in Gordon, 364.

32. Hansen in Yellin and VanHorne, eds., 45-49; Stanton, "Address to the Eighth National Woman's Rights Convention," May 13, 1858 in Gordon, 364.

33. ECS to GS, Aug. 3, 1840, SU.

34. Abby Kelley to GS, July 28, 1843, SU.

35. GS to Theodore Dwight Weld, Angelina and Sarah Grimké, July 11, 1840 in Wellman, 58.

36. See Kitch for more complete treatment of this theme.

37. This point will become clearer when we discuss the issue of woman suffrage in chapter 11.

38. HWS, I, 419; Kitch, 174; Robertson, 26.

39. Kitch, 80-81.

40. Harrold, 122-123.

41. Davis, 118-119; GS to ECS, Dec. 1, 1855, SU.

42. Colman, 124; Davis, 163-164; Banner, 106-107.

43. HWS, I, 476, 500-501, 848, 851.

44. Wellman, 132; Smith, T.L., 186-197.

45. ECS to ESM, Nov. 15, 1856 in Davis, 115.

46. Wagner, She Who..., 7; Griffith, 122; Abzug, Cosmos..., 223; Faulkner, 149.

47. HWS, II, 68-69.

48. ECS to GS, Dec. 16, 1861, SU; ECS to ESM, Aug. 11, 1862 in Davis, 116.

49. Friedman, 157.

50. ECS to the Editor of the National Anti-Slavery Standard, Dec. 26, 1865 in Gordon, 564.

51. New York Times, June 12, 1874.

Chapter 7

1. GS to ECS, Dec. 1, 1855, SU.

2. ECS to GS, Dec. 21, 1855, SU; Stanton, Eighty Years..., 158.

3. Frances D. Gage to Frederick Douglass, Dec. 24, 1855 in HWS, I, 842-843.

4. Sarah Grimké to GS in The Lily, Oct. 1, 1856.

5. Davis, 106; Stanton, Eighty Years..., 157; HWS, I, 470.

6. Wagner, <u>Sisters</u>…, 43; Lucy Stone to GS, Jan. 8, 1854, SU; Wellman, 222; Stanton, "Sobriny Jane" in Gordon, 179.

7. Frances D. Gage to Frederick Douglass, Dec. 24, 1855 in <u>HWS</u>, I, 855; <u>HWS</u>, I, 471; Stanton, <u>Eighty Years</u>…, 158.

8. <u>HWS</u>, I, 470-471.

9. <u>HWS</u>, I, 471; Colman, 75; Gordon, picture opposite p. 304.

10. Davis, 107; Banner, 107; Colman, 123.

11. GS to ECS, Dec. 1, 1855; ECS to GS, Dec. 21, 1855, SU.

12. Burdick, <u>Snipets</u>, vol. 2, 12.

13. <u>Frederick Douglass' Paper</u>, Dec. 28, 1855.

Chapter 8

1. ECS to SBA, March 1, 1852; ECS to Lucy Stone, Nov. 24, 1856 in Griffith, 102.

2. ECS to SBA, March 1, 1852 in Gordon, 194; Stanton, "Mrs. Dall's Fraternity Lecture," Nov. 16, 1860 in Gordon, 446-447.

3. Stanton, "Address to the Tenth National Woman's Rights Convention," May 11, 1860 in DuBois and Smith, eds., 186.

4. Stanton, "The Pivot…," in DuBois and Smith, eds., 86.

5. Wagner, <u>Sisters</u>…, 84-85; Davis, 81; Stanton, "Address to the Tenth National Woman's Rights Convention," May 11, 1860 in DuBous and Smith, eds., 184.

6. Stanton, "Divorce versus Domestic Warfare," in DuBois and Smith, eds., 256; Stanton, "Man Marriage," <u>The Revolution</u>, April 8, 1869, 218.

7. Faulkner, 160.

8. Griffith, 33; Stanton, <u>Eighty Years</u>…, 227.

9. <u>HWS</u>, I, 860; ECS to SBA, July 4, 1858 in Griffith, 95.

10. ECS to ESM, June 4, 1854 in Griffith, 87; ECS to SBA, Jan. 24, 1856 in Griffith, 88.

11. Griffith, 189; Banner, 109-111.

12. Davis, 71.

13. ECS to the editor of the New York Tribune, May 30, 1860 in HWS, I, 739.

14. Stanton, "Address to the Tenth National Woman's Rights Convention," May 11, 1860 in HWS, I, 718; ECS to GS, Dec. 21, 1855, SU.

15. Wellman, 146-148; Griffith, 43; DuBois, 4-5; Banner, 28-29.

16. Wellman, 149, 151.

17. Davis, 73; Wellman, 137; Ellis, et. al., 312.

18. Wagner, 64; Dann, Practical…, 376.

19. Stanton, "Address to the Tenth National Woman's Rights Convention," May 11, 1860 in DuBois and Smith, eds., 183; ECS to GS, Dec. 21, 1855, SU; Wagner, 48-49.

20. Stanton, Eighty Years…, 167; Stanton, "Address to the Tenth National Woman's Rights Convention," May 11, 1860 in DuBois and Smith, eds., 180; The Revolution, Dec. 23, 1869.

21. Griffith, 164, 104.

22. Stanton, Eighty Years…, 168.

23. DuBois, 97; Griffith, 102, 105.

24. Davis, 84; Griffith, 103; Colman, 89-91; Banner, 66-67; Gornick, "Elizabeth Cady Stanton, the Long View" in DuBois and Smith, eds., 21.

25. Smith, The Religion of Reason, 71.

26. Davis, 83; Smith, The Religion of Reason, 72-73.

27. Dann, Practical…, 190-191.

28. Stanton, Eighty Years…, 179-180.

29. ECS, "Divorce," The Lily, April 1850; Stanton, Eighty Years…, 179.

30. ECS, "Speech at McFarland-Richardson Protest Meeting," May, 1869 in DuBois, ed., 129-130.

31. Griffith, 102, 160.

32. GS to John Stuart Mill, Feb, 5, 1869, SU.

33. Griffith, 106, 249n; Davis, 85-89, 80, 91.

34. ECS to GS, Dec. 21, 1855, SU.

Chapter 9

1. Stanton, <u>Eighty Years</u>…, 29-30, 41-42.

2. Lucretia Mott to ECS, March 23, 1841 in Wellman, 163; Stanton, <u>Eighty Years</u>…, 30, 43.

3. Dann, <u>Practical</u>…, 230.

4. Wellman, 163-164; Dann, <u>Practical</u>…, 260.

5. Dann, <u>Practical</u>…, 261-272.

6. DuBois, ed., 243; Stanton, <u>Eighty Years</u>…, 49-50.

7. Stanton, "The Matriarchate, or Mother Age," in DuBois and Smith, eds., 265-267.

8. Davis, 265; Wagner, 18.

9. Stanton, <u>Eighty Years</u>…, 271, 289; Stanton, "The Matriarchate, or Mother Age," in DuBois and Smith, eds., 274.

10. Griffith, 78; Davis, 67; Stanton, "The Woman's Bible," in DuBois and Smith, eds., 288; Stanton, <u>Eighty Years</u>…, 229; Stanton, "Perhaps," in Gordon, 109.

11. Wagner, <u>Sisters</u>…, 50; Wagner, <u>Matilda</u>…, 40, 57, 58.

12. Grube; Stanton, "Home Life," in DuBois, ed., 136.

13. <u>HWS</u>, I, 543; Colman, 35; Wagner, <u>Matilda</u>…, 40-41.

14. Stanton, "The Woman's Bible," in DuBois and Smith, eds., 284; Antoinette L. Brown to GS, Dec. 26, 1851, SU.

15. Banner, 157; <u>HWS</u>, IV, xxiv.

16. Warren, 2; Humphreys.

17. Dann, <u>Practical</u>…, 261.

18. DuBois, 228-229; Davis, 102, 185; Stanton, <u>Eighty Years</u>…, 300.

19. Stanton, <u>Eighty Years</u>…, 295; Banner, 163; Faulkner, 156;

Griffith, 210-212.

20. Stanton, The Woman's Bible, in DuBois and Smith, eds., 282-283.

21. GS to E.G. Messinger, March 4, 1848, SU; Stanton, "The Slave's Appeal."

22. Stanton, "Address to the American Anti-Slavery Society," May 8, 1860, in DuBois, ed., 80.

23. Wellman, 128-130; Newman, Freedom's..., 53, 173-174.

24. Newman, Freedom's...,179, 232.

25. Stanton, Eighty Years..., 219-220.

Chapter 10

1. Stanton, Eighty Years..., 149.

2. Wellman, 176; Faulkner, 138.

3. GS to Judge Nye, July 27, 1848, SU; GS to The Rank and File of the Democratic Party, Oct. 20, 1864, SU.

4. GS to Josiah Spalding, Jan. 5, 1846, SU; GS to the Albany Patriot, May 8, 1847, SU; GS to Alvan Stewart, July 20, 1840, SU; HWS, I, 473.

5. Wellman, 160-161, 170-172, 177-182.

6. Colman, 108-109; Gordon, 593; ACS to ECS, Oct. 21, 1866 in Gordon, 596-597; Stanton, "Speech at Lawrence, Kansas," in DuBois, ed., 117; Davis, 47-48.

7. Stanton, "Proposal to form a New Party," in DuBois, ed., 167.

8. HWS, II, 516-517, 517n.

9. ECS to SBA, Nov. 4, 1855 in Griffith, 90; Griffith, 67; Davis, 115.

10. HWS, I, 676; Davis, 125; Banner, 100-101; Stanton, editorial in The Revolution, Feb. 12, 1869.

Chapter 11

1. Wagner, Matilda..., 28.
2. Stanton, "Address to AERA," May 12, 1869, in DuBois and Smith, eds., 192.
3. HWS, III, vi.
4. HWS, II, 266; Stanton, "Gerrit Smith on Petitions," in DuBois, ed., 120.
5. Lemons, 13; Wagner, Sisters..., 81; ECS to Lucretia Mott, July 19, 1876 in HWS, III, 45.
6. Wellman, 141; Foner, Eric, 14-16.
7. Colman, 105-106; Davis, 131.
8. Robertson, 142, 153; Faulkner, 191; Lemons, 47-49.
9. Faulkner, 195; Douglass, speech at AERA Convention, May 12-14, 1869 in HWS, II, 382.
10. GS to Susan B. Anthony, Dec. 30, 1868, SU; Smith, "On Suffrage," speech in Albany, Feb. 28, 1856, SLC; Dann, Practical..., 373-374.
11. ECS to the National Anti-Slavery Standard, Dec. 30, 1865 in Robertson, 140; Robertson, 136.
12. Mayer, 609; Gordon, 587.
13. Davis, 135; HWS, II, 323.
14. HWS, II, 281, 304-305; Banner, 95.
15. HWS, II, 351; Griffith, 119.
16. HWS, II, 320; GS to William Lloyd Garrison and Wendell Phillips, Sept. 12, 1865, SLC; GS to Everett Brown, Aug. 9, 1872, SLC.
17. HWS, II, 316-318.
18. SBA to GS, March 3, 1867, SU; GS to SBA, Dec. 30, 1868, SU.
19. ECS to GS, April 10, 1865, SU; HWS, II, 318.
20. HWS, IV, 435; Faulkner, 215; HWS, II, 322.

21. The Revolution, Jan. 14, 1869; Griffith, 134; Foner, Philip, 600.
22. Faulkner, 187; Davis, 137-138.
23. DuBois, ed., 90; HWS, II, 1.
24. HWS, II, 320; The Revolution, Dec. 6, 1869.
25. Davis, 26-27.
26. Faulkner, 188; Gordon, 104-105.
27. Lemons, 36-37; Stanton, Eighty Years…, 243; The Revolution, Dec. 24, 1868.
28. HWS, II, 94; Mayer, 607.
29. HWS, II, 214.
30. Lemons, 36; Williams, "The Female Antislavery Movement," in Yellin and VanHorne, eds., 166-167.
31. Griffith, 123; Stanton, Eighty Years…, 186-189; Colman, 106.
32. Griffith, 148, 155.
33. HWS, II, 334-335; Anthony, "Homes of Single Women," Oct., 1877 in DuBois, ed., 163.
34. Gornick, "Elizabeth Cady Stanton, the Long View" in DuBois and Smith, eds., 25; Stanton, "Address to the Founding Convention of NAWSA," Feb., 1890 in DuBois, ed., 226.
35. Wagner, Sisters…, 16; Stanton, Eighty Years…, 155.
36. HWS, I, 14; HWS, IV, xiv, xxiii.
37. Davis, 66; Stanton, Eighty Years…, 284-285.
38. Davis, 64; HWS, II, 225; Stanton, "Address to the AERA, May 12, 1869 in DuBois and Smith, eds., 204; Gordon, 108.
39. Wellman, 145; Davis, 56-57.
40. Wyatt-Brown, 191-193; HWS, I, 61-62.
41. Wyatt-Brown, 197-198.
42. Wellman, 193; Davis, 56; HWS, IV, 1; Wellman, 214.
43. Foner, Eric, 39; Robertson, 57; Wellman, 152.
44. Smith, speech in Buffalo, SLC; Faulkner, 138; Wellman, 176; web site 1.

45. Wellman, 217; ECS to GS, July 3, 1864, SU.

46. Colman, 96-97; Griffith, 108-110.

47. Stanton, Eighty Years…, 230.

48. Griffith, 118-119; Davis, 129; HWS, II, 281.

49. Stanton, Eighty Years…, 186; Robertson, 142-144; HWS, II, 342n.

50. Robertson, 141, 153-154; Bacon, 165, 211-212.

51. HWS, II, 923-924, 98.

52. Higginson to SBA, May 14, 1866 in HWS, II, 917, 89; Davis, 66-67.

53. ECS to GS, Jan. 1, 1866, SU; Colman, 139.

54. Kitch, 184; Wellman, 138; HWS, II, 277.

55. Banner, 96; HWS, III, 427; HWS, IV, 861; HWS, V, xxiii.

56. ECS to ESM, Dec. 14, 1867 in Griffith, 128; Banner, 98-101; Davis, 133; Colman, 114; HWS, II, 230, 265.

57. HWS, III, 727; HWS, V, 634.

58. Griffith, 138-140; Wagner, Matilda…, 50.

59. Davis, 161-162, 182-184.

60. HWS, II, 333.

61. Wagner, Matilda…, 28; Griffith, 192.

62. Banner, 138-139; Stanton, Eighty Years…, 276-281, 290-291; ECS to SBA, Aug. 18, 1880 in Griffith, 171; Colman, 187-188.

63. Wagner, Sisters…, 81; DuBois, ed., 107; Davis, 158; Wagner, Matilda…, 14; Banner, 141; Colman, 182, 197; HWS, III, iv.

64. DuBois, ed., 103; Colman, 150-152.

65. Faulkner, 207; Griffith, 154; HWS, II, 647, 689, 691, 700.

66. Colman, 154.

67. HWS, II, 714.

68. GS to Mrs. Howe and Lucy Stone, Nov. 15, 1872 in HWS, II, 825; GS to SBA, Aug. 15, 1873, SLC.

69. GS to SBA, Feb. 5, 1873, SLC.

70. GS to SBA, Aug. 15, 1873, SLC.

71. Griffith, 217.

72. Hicks, et. al., xvii; <u>HWS</u>, V, xxiii-xxiv.

73. <u>HWS</u>, V, 594.

Epilogue

1. Sklar, "Women Who Speak for an Entire Nation" in Yellin and Van Horne, eds., 301n; Davis, 117; Colman, 203.

2. <u>HWS</u>, II, 267.

3. Manning, A-2.

4. Deam, 29-38.

5. Manning, A-2; ABC News, Feb. 12, 2012; ABC News, October 13, 2011; <u>The Post Standard</u>, March 23, 2012, A-12.

6. ECS to SBA, April 27, 1898 in DuBois, ed., 288; Stauffer, 238-239.

7. ABC News, February 16, 2012.

8. Beck, 79.

Bibliography

<u>Books</u>

Abzug, Robert H. <u>Cosmos Crumbling: American Reform and the Religious Imagination</u>, New York: Oxford University Press, 1994.

---- <u>Passionate Liberator: Theodore Dwight Weld and the Dilemma of Reform</u>, New York: Oxford University Press, 1980.

Allen, Paula Gunn. <u>The Sacred Hoop: Recovering the Feminine in American Indian Traditions</u>, Boston: Beacon Press, 1986.

<u>Ayer's American Almanac</u>, for the use of Farmers, Planters, Mechanics, Mariners, and All Families. Lowell: Dr. J.C. Ayer + Co., Practical and Analytical Chemists, 1870.

Bacon, Margaret Hope. <u>But One Race: The Life of Robert Purvis</u>, Albany: State University of New York Press, 2007.

Baker, Jean H. <u>Sisters: The Lives of America's Suffragists</u>, New York: Hill and Wang, 2005.

Banner, Lois W. <u>Elizabeth Cady Stanton: A Radical for Woman's Rights</u>, Boston: Little, Brown and Company, 1980.

Beck, Janet Kemper. <u>Creating the John Brown Legend</u>, North Carolina: McFarland + Company, 2009.

Braude, Ann. Radical Spirits: Spiritualism and Women's Rights in Nineteenth Century America, Boston: Beacon Press, 1989.

Burdick, Donna Dorrance. Snipets, vol. 2, unpublished manuscript, 1995.

---- "'Spirited' Women in Peterboro," Historic CNY, Fall, 2003, 9-11.

Child, Lydia Maria. An Appeal In Favor of that Class of Americans Called Africans, Bedford: Applewood Books, originally published in 1833.

Colman, Penny. Elizabeth Cady Stanton and Susan B. Anthony: A Friendship that Changed the World, New York: Henry Holt and Company, 2011.

Dann, Norman K. Practical Dreamer: Gerrit Smith and the Crusade for Social Reform, Hamilton: Log Cabin Books, 2009.

---- Whatever it Takes: The Antislavery Movement and the Tactics of Gerrit Smith, Hamilton: Log Cabin Books, 2011.

---- When We Get to Heaven: Runaway Slaves on the Road to Peterboro, Hamilton: Log Cabin Books, 2008.

Davis, Sue. The Political Thought of Elizabeth Cady Stanton: Women's Rights and the American Political Traditions, New York: New York University Press, 2008.

Douglass, Frederick. Life and Times of Frederick Douglass, Hartford: Park Publishing Co., 1881.

DuBois, Ellen Carol and Richard Candida Smith, eds., Elizabeth Cady Stanton, Feminist as Thinker, New York: New York University Press, 2007.

Ellis, David et al., A Short History of New York State, Ithaca: Cornell University Press, 1957.

Faulkner, Carol. Lucretia Mott's Heresy: Abolition and Women's Rights in Nineteenth-Century America, Philadelphia: University of Pennsylvania, 2011.

Foner, Eric. The Fiery Trial: Abraham Lincoln and American Slavery, New York: W.W. Norton, 2010.

Foner, Philip S., ed., Frederick Douglass: Selected Speeches and Writings, Chicago: Lawrence Hill Books, 1999.

Friedman Lawrence J. Gregarious Saints: Self and Community in American Abolitionism, 1830-1870. Cambridge: Cambridge University Press, 1982.

Frothingham, Octavius Brooks. Gerrit Smith, 1ˢᵗ ed., New York: G.P. Putnam's Sons, 1878.

George-Kanentiio, Doug. Iroquois Culture + Commentary, Santa Fe: Clear Light Publishers, 2000.

Gordon, Ann et al., eds. The Selected Papers of Elizabeth Cady Stanton and Susan B. Anthony, vol. 1, New Brunswick: Rutgers University Press, 1997.

Griffith, Elisabeth. In Her Own Right: The Life of Elizabeth Cady Stanton, New York: Oxford University Press, 1984.

Grube, Melinda. "Matilda Joslyn Gage: Challenging the Religious Right," Fayetteville: Matilda Joslyn Gage Foundation, 2008.

Harrold, Stanley. Border War: Fighting Over Slavery Before the Civil War, Chapel Hill: University of North Carolina Press, 2010.

Hicks, John D., George E. Mowry, and Robert E. Burke. The Federal Union, 4th ed., Boston: Houghton Mifflin Company, 1964.

Hodges, Graham Russell Gao. David Ruggles, Chapel Hill: The University of North Carolina Press, 2010.

Humphreys, Hugh C. Agitate! Agitate! Agitate!: The Great Fugitive Slave Law Convention and its Rare Daguerreotype, Oneida: Madison County Historical Society, 1994.

Kern, Kathi. Mrs. Stanton's Bible, Ithaca: Cornell University Press, 2001.

Kitch, Sally L. The Specter of Sex: Gendered Foundations of Racial Formation in the United States, Albany: SUNY Press, 2009.

Lemons, Gary L. Womanist Forefathers: Frederick Douglass and W.E.B. DuBois, Albany: SUNY Press, 2009.

Letters and Addresses of George Thompson, New York: Negro Universities Press, 1969. Originally published in 1837.

Macionis, John J. Sociology, 7th ed., Upper Saddle River: Prentice Hall, 1999.

Mayer, Henry. All on Fire: William Lloyd Garrison and the Abolition of Slavery, New York: St. Martin's Press, 1998.

McFeely, William S. Frederick Douglass, New York: W.W. Norton + Company, 1991.

Newman, Richard S. Freedom's Prophet: Bishop Richard Allen, the AME Church, and the Black Founding Fathers, New York: New York University Press, 2008.

Robertson, Stacey M. Parker Pillsbury: Radical Abolitionist, Male Feminist, Ithaca: Cornell University Press, 2000.

Sernett, Milton C. Harriet Tubman: Myth, Memory, and History, Durham: Duke University Press, 2007.

Smith, Gerrit. The Religion of Reason, New York: Ross + Tousey, 1859.

Smith, Timothy L. Revivalism and Social Reform: American Protestantism on the Eve of the Civil War, Baltimore: The Johns Hopkins University Press, 1980.

Stanton, Elizabeth Cady. Eighty Years and More: Reminiscences 1815-1897, Bibliobazaar edition, 2006. Originally published in 1898.

Stanton, Elizabeth Cady, Susan B. Anthony, Matilda Joslyn Gage, eds., History of Woman Suffrage, vol. I-III; Susan B. Anthony and Ida Husted Harper, eds., vol. IV; Ida Husted Harper, ed., vol. V + VI, New York: Source Book Press, 1881-1922.

Stauffer, John. Giants: The Parallel Lives of Frederick Douglass + Abraham Lincoln, New York: Twelve, 2008.

Sterling, Dorothy. Ahead of Her Time: Abby Kelley and the Politics of Antislavery, New York: W.W. Norton + Co., 1991.

Tyler, Alice Felt. Freedom's Ferment, New York: Harper and Row, 1962.

Ulrich, Laurel Thatcher. Well-Behaved Women Seldom Make History, New York: Vintage Books, 2007.

Wagner, Sally Roesch. Matilda Joslyn Gage: She Who Holds the Sky, Aberdeen: Sky Carrier Press, 2002.

---- Sisters in Spirit: Haudenosaunee (Iroquois) Influence on Early American Feminists, Summertown, Tennessee: Native Voices, 2001.

Warren, James Perrin. Culture of Eloquence: Oratory and Reform in Antebellum America, University Park: The Pennsylvania State University Press, 1999.

Wellman, Judith. The Road to Seneca Falls: Elizabeth Cady Stanton and the First Woman's Rights Convention, Chicago: University of Illinois Press, 2004.

Wyatt-Brown, Bertram. Lewis Tappan and the Evangelical War Against Slavery, Baton Rouge: Louisiana State University Press, 1969.

Yellin, Jean Fagan and John C. Van Horne, eds., The Abolitionist Sisterhood: Women's Political Culture in Antebellum America, Ithaca: Cornell University Press, 1994.

Periodicals

The Des Moines Register, Oct. 20. 2008.

Frederick Douglass' Paper, Dec. 22, 1854; Dec. 28, 1855.

The Liberator, Sept. 6, 1834; March 27, 1846; March 1, 1850.

The Lily, April 1850; Oct. 1856.

New York Times, June 12, 1874; Oct. 27, 1902.

The North Star, July 28, 1848.

Oneida Whig, Aug, 1, 1848.

The Revolution, Dec. 24, 1868; Jan. 14, 1869; Feb. 12, 1869; April 8, 1869; April 14, 1869; Dec. 6, 1869; Dec. 23, 1869.

Seneca County Courier, July 23, 1848.

The State League, Aug. 25, 1860.

Western Citizen, Aug. 24, 1847.

Articles

Anthony, Susan B. "Homes of Single Women," Oct. 1877 in Ellen Carol DuBois, ed., The Elizabeth Cady Stanton-Susan B. Anthony Reader, Boston: Northeastern University Press, 1981.

Davis, Mary B. "For the Western Citizen," in Western Citizen, Aug. 24, 1847.

Deam, Jenny. "Preexisting Condition: Female," Prevention, Dec. 2011, 29-38.

DuBois, Ellen Carol. "The Pivot of the Marriage Relation: Stanton's Analysis of Women's Subordination in Marriage," in DuBois and Smith, eds., Elizabeth Cady Stanton: Feminist as Thinker, New York: New York University Press, 2007.

Ecker, Sydney W. "Brain Gender Identity," 2009, at aebrain. blogspot.com/2009/05/brain-gender-identity-presentation-by.html

Gage, Matilda Joslyn. "The Foundation of Sovereignty," Woman's Tribune, April 1887.

Gornick, Vivian. "Elizabeth Cady Stanton, the Long View" in DuBois and Smith, eds., Elizabeth Cady Stanton: Feminist as Thinker, New York: New York University Press, 2007.

Hansen, Debra Gold. "The Boston Female Anti-Slavery Society and the Limits of Gender Politics," in Jean Fagan Yellin and John C. Van Horne, eds., The Abolitionist Sisterhood, Ithaca: Cornell University Press, 1994.

Hewitt, Nancy A. "On Their Own Terms," in Jean Fagan Yellin and John C. Van Horne, The Abolitionist Sisterhood, Ithaca: Cornell University Press, 1994.

Kern, Kathi. "Free Woman Is a Divine Being, the Savior of Mankind: Stanton's Exploration of Religion and Gender," in DuBois and Smith, eds., Elizabeth Cady Stanton: Feminist as Thinker, New York: New York University Press, 2007.

Manning, Sue. "Steinem: Where Women Are Now," The Post Standard, March 11, 2012, A-2.

Mesinger, Judith. "The Feminist Movement as Reflected in the Gerrit Smith Papers," The Courier, Syracuse University Press, Fall 1973.

Petrulinois, Sandra. "Swelling That Great Tide of Humanity," The New England Quarterly, 74:3, 2001.

Phrenological Reports-1853, in Ellen Carol DuBois, ed., The Elizabeth Cady Stanton-Susan B. Anthony Readers, Boston: Northeastern University Press, 1981.

Sklar, Kathryn Kish. "Women Who Speak for and Entire Nation: American and British Women at the World Anti-Slavery Convention, London, 1840," in Jean Fagan Yellin and John C. Van Horne, The Abolitionist Sisterhood, Ithaca: Cornell University Press, 1994.

Smith, Gerrit. "The Crime of the Abolitionists," Oct. 22, 1835.

---- "Woman's War Upon the Dramshops," March 24, 1874.

Soderlund, Jean R. "Priorities and Power," in Jean Fagan Yellin and John C. Van Horne, The Abolitionist Sisterhood, Ithaca: Cornell University Press, 1994.

Stanton, Elizabeth Cady. "Address Delivered at Seneca Falls," July 19, 1848 in Ellen Carol DuBois, ed., The Elizabeth Cady Stanton-

Susan B. Anthony Reader, Boston: Northeastern University Press, 1981.

---- "Address of Welcome to the International Council of Women," March 25, 1880 in Ellen Carol DuBois, ed., The Elizabeth Cady Stanton-Susan B. Anthony Reader, Boston: Northeastern University Press, 1981.

---- "Address to AERA, May 12, 1869" in DuBois and Smith, eds., Elizabeth Cady Stanton: Feminist as Thinker, New York: New York University Press, 2007.

---- "Address to the Founding Convention of the NAWSA, February 1890" in Ellen Carol DuBois, ed., The Elizabeth Cady Stanton-Susan B. Anthony Reader, Boston: Northeastern University Press, 1981.

---- "Address to the Legislature of New York on Women's Rights," Feburary 14, 1854 in Ellen Carol DuBois, ed., The Elizabeth Cady Stanton-Susan B. Anthony Reader, Boston: Northeastern University Press, 1981.

---- "Divorce versus Domestic Warfare," 1890 in DuBois and Smith, eds., Elizabeth Cady Stanton: Feminist as Thinker, New York: New York University Press, 2007.

---- "Has Christianity Benefited Woman?" 1885 in DuBois and Smith, eds., Elizabeth Cady Stanton: Feminist as Thinker, New York: New York University Press, 2007.

---- "Home Life," 1875 in Ellen Carol DuBois, ed., The Elizabeth Cady Stanton-Susan B. Anthony Reader, Boston: Northeastern University Press, 1981.

---- "Man Marriage," The Revolution, April 8, 1869.

---- "The Matriarchate, or Mother-Age," 1891 in DuBois and Smith, eds., Elizabeth Cady Stanton: Feminist as Thinker, New York: New York University Press, 2007.

---- "The Other Side of the Woman Question," 1879 in DuBois and Smith, eds., Elizabeth Cady Stanton: Feminist as Thinker, New York: New York University Press, 2007.

---- "Proposal to Form a New Party," in Ellen Carol DuBois, ed., The Elizabeth Cady Stanton-Susan B. Anthony Reader, Boston: Northeastern University Press, 1981.

---- "Selections from The Woman's Bible" in DuBois and Smith, eds., Elizabeth Cady Stanton: Feminist as Thinker, New York: New York University Press, 2007.

---- "The Slave's Appeal," pamphlet published by the Anti-Slavery Depository, Albany, New York, 1860.

---- "The Solitude of Self" in Ellen Carol DuBois, ed., The Elizabeth Cady Stanton-Susan B. Anthony Reader, Boston: Northeastern University Press, 1981.

---- "Speech at Lawrence, Kansas," 1867 in Ellen Carol DuBois, ed., The Elizabeth Cady Stanton-Susan B. Anthony Reader, Boston: Northeastern University Press, 1981.

---- "Speech to the Anniversary of the American Anti-Slavery Society," 1860 in Ellen Carol DuBois, ed., The Elizabeth Cady

Stanton-Susan B. Anthony Reader, Boston: Northeastern University Press, 1981.

---- "Speech to the McFarland-Richardson Protest Meeting," May, 1869 in Ellen Carol DuBois, ed., The Elizabeth Cady Stanton-Susan B. Anthony Reader, Boston: Northeastern University Press, 1981.

---- "Subjection of Women," 1875 in DuBois and Smith, eds., Elizabeth Cady Stanton: Feminist as Thinker, New York: New York University Press, 2007.

Stauffer, John. "Beyond Social Control: The Example of Gerrit Smith, Romantic Radical," ATQ, Sept. 1997, 233-259.

Swerdlow, Amy. "Abolition's Conservative Sisters," in Jean Fagan Yellin and John C. Van Horne, eds., The Abolitionist Sisterhood, Ithaca: Cornell University Press, 1994.

Williams, Carolyn. "The Female Antislavery Movement," in Jean Fagan Yellin and John C. Van Horne, eds., The Abolitionist Sisterhood, Ithaca: Cornell University Press, 1994.

Web Sites

1. http://www.viswiki.com/en/gerrit_smith
2. http://www.historyplace.com/speeches/stanton/htm
3. http://www.voicesofdemocracy.umd.edu/justice/stanton1880txt. xml
4. http://www.wwhp.org/news-events/news-articles/2012/abby-kelley-foster-inducted…2/18/2012

Index

Index

Index

Index

Index

About the Author

This is the fourth book by Norman K. Dann, Ph.D.

He was born in Providence, RI in 1940. After graduating from Mt. Pleasant High School, he spent three years in the U.S. Navy as an aviation electronics technician.

He earned a bachelor of arts degree in psychology from Alderson-Broaddus College in Philippi, WV and a master of arts in Political Science from the University of Rhode Island.

He was graduated from Syracuse University in 1974 with a Ph.D. in Interdisciplinary Social Sciences. In 1999, he retired after 33 years on the faculty of the Social Sciences Department at Morrisville State College.

In retirement, Norm has specialized in research and writing on the abolition movement, with several articles and book reviews in publication. He published his first book, *When We Get to Heaven: Runaway Slaves on the Road to Peterboro*, in 2008. His second book in 2009 was a full biography that capped more than 15 years of research on abolitionist Gerrit Smith. It is titled *Practical Dreamer: Gerrit Smith and the Crusade for Social Reform*. His third book, *Whatever It Takes: The Antislavery Movement and the Tactics of Gerrit Smith*, came out in 2011. All titles are from Log Cabin Books of Hamilton, NY.

His other interests include sterling silver craft work. He creates jewelry pieces and specializes in silver plaques. One plaque was a centerpiece of Madison County's bicentennial celebration in 2006. Norm also enjoys archery hunting for whitetail deer and maintains a large vegetable garden. He cultivates hop plants for display and sale through the annual Madison County Hop Fest.

Norm has dedicated his retirement to communicating the importance of local history regarding abolition. He is a member of the Peterboro-based Smithfield Community Association and helps manage the group's annual fund-raiser, Civil War Weekend. He is a founding member of the National Abolition Hall of Fame & Museum.

Other Books by Norman K. Dann

When We Get to Heaven:
Runaway Slaves on the Road to Peterboro
(2008)

Practical Dreamer:
Gerrit Smith and the Crusade for Social Reform
(2009)

Whatever It Takes:
The Antislavery Movement
and the Tactics of Gerrit Smith
(2011)

Greene Smith and the WildLife:
The Story of Peterboro's Avid Outdoorsman
(2015)

All titles are from
LOG CABIN BOOKS of Hamilton, NY.
www.logcabinbooks.com